Rāmopākhyāna

The story of Rāma in the Mahābhārata
A close English prose translation

PETER M. SCHARF

20 December 2023

Scharf, Peter M. *Rāmopākhyāna: the story of Rāma in the Mahābhārata: a close English prose translation.* Providence: The Sanskrit Library, 2023.

Library of Congress Control Number: 2023922038

ISBN: 978-1-943135-12-7

The Sanskrit Library
89 Cole Avenue
Providence, RI 02906
USA
sanskritlibrary.org

Preface

The purpose of this publication is to contribution to broadening the enjoyment and understanding of the literature and culture of India by making the classical Indian story of Rāma available to a wider audience. Just last month I completed the revised editions of my *Rāmopakhyāna* published in 2002. That text was intended as an independent-study reader or intermediate Sanskrit textbook for students of Sanskrit. The revised edition is issued in a version with all the Sanskrit in Devanāgarī as well as in a version with the Sanskrit in the analysis and notes Romanized and just the verse and prose paraphrases of it in Devanāgarī. The present publication makes the translation, together with selections from the introduction and appendices, available to an audience that does not read Sanskrit and is not studying Sanskrit. It is therefore suitable for the general reader as well as for university and secondary school classes that introduce Indian literature, religion, and culture.

Table of contents

Preface . . . . **iii**

Table of contents . . . . **v**

List of tables. . . . . **ix**

Introduction 1

I. Divine, historical, and spiritual dimensions. **3**
- A. The story of Rāma 4
  - 1. The human dimension 4
  - 2. The divine dimension 5
- B. The *Rāmopākhyāna*. 6
- C. Textual limits to the divine dimension 7
  - 1. Limits in the *Rāmāyaṇa* 8
  - 2. Limits in the *Rāmopākhyāna* 9
- D. Rāma and Sītā's humanity. 11
  - 1. Human emotions, intelligence, etc. 11
  - 2. Rāma's ethics 12
    - a. The mutilation of Śūrpaṇakhā 12
    - b. The slaying of Vālin 13
    - c. The rejection of Sītā 13
- E. Moral versus mundane factors in Sītā's rejection 15
- F. Moral revisionism in narrative adaptation 18
  - 1. Parallels to Sītā's case 20
  - 2. Comparison of Yudhiṣṭhira's and Rāma's exiles . . 21
- G. The historical basis 22
  - 1. The monkeys 22
- H. The spiritual dimension 24
  - 1. Various classes of beings. 24
  - 2. Siddhis 25

3. Transcending and enlightenment 30

II. A note on the text and translation 33

Translation 35

Mahābhārata Āraṇyakaparvan, Adhyāya 257
Yudhiṣṭhira's lament over the abduction of Kṛṣṇā 37

Mahābhārata Āraṇyakaparvan, Adhyāya 258; Rāmopākhyāna, Adhyāya 1
The birth of Rāma and Rāvaṇa 39

Mahābhārata Āraṇyakaparvan, Adhyāya 259; Rāmopākhyāna, Adhyāya 2
The obtainment of boons by Rāvaṇa and his siblings 41

Mahābhārata Āraṇyakaparvan, Adhyāya 260; Rāmopākhyāna, Adhyāya 3
The birth of the gods in the form of monkeys and bears. . . . 45

Mahābhārata Āraṇyakaparvan, Adhyāya 261; Rāmopākhyāna, Adhyāya 4
The departure of Rāma, Lakṣmaṇa, and Sitā to the forest . . 47

Mahābhārata Āraṇyakaparvan, Adhyāya 262; Rāmopākhyāna, Adhyāya 5
The slaying of Mārīca and abduction of Sītā 53

Mahābhārata Āraṇyakaparvan, Adhyāya 263; Rāmopākhyāna, Adhyāya 6
The slaying of Kabandha 57

Mahābhārata Āraṇyakaparvan, Adhyāya 264; Rāmopākhyāna, Adhyāya 7
The consolation of Sītā by Trijaṭā 61

Mahābhārata Āraṇyakaparvan, Adhyāya 265; Rāmopākhyā-na, Adhyāya 8
The dialogue between Sītā and Rāvaṇa 67

Mahābhārata Āraṇyakaparvan, Adhyāya 266; Rāmopākhyā-na, Adhyāya 9
The return of Hanūmat 71

Mahābhārata Āraṇyakaparvan, Adhyāya 267; Rāmopākhyā-na, Adhyāya 10
The building of the bridge to Laṅkā. 77

Mahābhārata Āraṇyakaparvan, Adhyāya 268; Rāmopākhyā-na, Adhyāya 11
The first assault on Laṅkā. 81

Mahābhārata Āraṇyakaparvan, Adhyāya 269; Rāmopākhyā-na, Adhyāya 12
The battle between the pairs Rāma and Rāvaṇa, etc. 85

Mahābhārata Āraṇyakaparvan, Adhyāya 270; Rāmopākhyā-na, Adhyāya 13
The emergence of Kumbhakarṇa 87

Mahābhārata Āraṇyakaparvan, Adhyāya 271; Rāmopākhyā-na, Adhyāya 14
The slaying of Kumbhakarṇa, Vajravega and Pramāthin . . . 91

Mahābhārata Āraṇyakaparvan, Adhyāya 272; Rāmopākhyā-na, Adhyāya 15
Indrajit's felling of Rāma and Lakṣmaṇa 95

Mahābhārata Āraṇyakaparvan, Adhyāya 273; Rāmopākhyā-na, Adhyāya 16
Lakṣmaṇa's slaying of Indrajit 99

Mahābhārata Āraṇyakaparvan, Adhyāya 274; Rāmopākhyāna, Adhyāya 17
Rāma's slaying of Rāvaṇa 103

Mahābhārata Āraṇyakaparvan, Adhyāya 275; Rāmopākhyāna, Adhyāya 18
Rāma's reunion with Sītā, return to Ayodhyā and consecration 107

Mahābhārata Āraṇyakaparvan, Adhyāya 276
Mārkaṇḍeya's encouragement of Yudhiṣṭhira 113

Appendices 115

A. Glossary of proper names 117

B. Genealogy 151

C. Bibliography 153
1. Related books by the author 153
2. Critical editions of the epics 153
3. English translations of the epics 153
4. Production in audiovisual media 154
5. Research on the story of Rāma 155
6. Other references 164

List of tables

Introduction

I

Divine, historical, and spiritual dimensions of the story of Rāma, and its place in the *Mahābhārata*

The story of Rāma is a rich, multi-dimensional, multi-layered, organic narrative fabric. Alive and growing, it has and continues to incorporate, embody, and represent the cultural life of the countless redactors who have contributed threads to the various dimensions of the story. Three prominent dimensions interwoven in the story are the human drama of a man overcoming deprivation and sorrow by rescuing his abducted wife and slaying her abductor in battle, the divine victory of the gods over the demons won on the human battlefield, and the spiritual enlightenment of the individual self realizing its unbounded nature.

As one compares various versions of the story with each other, one can distinguish the threads of the human, divine, and spiritual dimensions unique to each redaction. One can segregate these strands even in the earliest extant layers of the narrative, namely in the *Rāmāyaṇa* and the *Rāmopākhyāna* of the *Mahābhārata*, where the expectation that Rāma is divine hasn't been thoroughly imposed on the text. By analyzing the narrative one can unravel supplementary strands to isolate and identify the original thread of plot around which the others have built. While this exercise leads one to identify the human dimension of the story as historically prior, one must recognize that its sythesis with the divine dimension accounts for its continuing popularity and survival. The anthropomorphic divine dimension, in turn, at once distinct from the more abstract spiritual dimension of the story, illuminates the perennial spiritual knowledge which resonates with life and vibrancy in much of Indian literature.

A. The story of Rāma

The story of Rāma is the most popular story in all of India and a masterpiece of world literature. In its most ancient extant version, it is told in Vālmīki's large epic poem *Rāmāyaṇa*, itself composed over several centuries and reaching its present shape by the 4th century C.E. Before the final redaction of the *Rāmāyaṇa*, however, it is summarized in the *Rāmopākhyāna* in the great epic *Mahābhārata*, composed over a longer period, beginning a century earlier and reaching its present shape about a century later.[1] More than 35 other major Sanskrit works retell the story of Rāma, including historical compilations, narratives, dramas, and philosophical treatises. Numerous versions in every modern Indian language and those of Southeast Asia also retell it. The religious cultures of Jainism, Buddhism and Islam have adopted it, and through Buddhist affiliations there arose Tibetan and Khotanese versions. As stories of an unnamed king, it was redacted in two full Chinese versions dating to 251 and 472 C.E. and later in Japanese versions as early as the 12th century. The story continues to be retold in both traditional and contemporary media. It is reenacted every autumn in Ramnagar and Varanasi in the ten-day outdoor dramatic performance *Rāmalīlā* culminating in Rāma's victory on Victory Day (*vijayadaśamī*). It was made into a movie, and, in 1987–88, into a television series which captured the attention of the Indian people to such an extent that business ceased and the streets were deserted during the hour it aired. The television series was reproduced twice and rebroadcast several times in several languages. As a glance at the bibliography reveals, research continues to trace the creative adaptation and global spread of the popular narrative.

1. The human dimension

The story begins in Ayodhyā where king Daśaratha lives with his three wives (Kausalyā, Kaikeyī, and Sumitrā), and four sons (Rāma,

[1] See J. L. Brockington 1978 etc.

Bharata, Lakṣmaṇa, and Śatrughna). When Kaikeyī learns that her husband is preparing to consecrate Kausalyā's son Rāma as crown-prince, she asks the king to fulfill the wish he had promised her when she saved his life, a wish she had deferred. Upon his assent, she requests that her son Bharata be consecrated crown-prince instead of Rāma and that Rāma be banished to the forest. Although the king remains silent, Rāma departs for the forest immediately to preserve his father's word. He is accompanied by his wife Sītā and Sumitrā's elder son Lakṣmaṇa. His father dies in grief at his departure, and Kaikeyī's son Bharata, for whom his mother made the request in his absence, refuses the crown and sets out to bring Rāma back. When Rāma refuses to return out of insistence to carry out the word of their father, Bharata sympathetically adopts the life of a spiritual practitioner, exiles himself to a small village, and rules the kingdom in Rāma's name from there. Rāma enters Daṇḍaka's forest where he dwells with Sītā and Lakṣmaṇa in a hermitage on the bank of the Godāvarī River. There he slays Rākṣasas, including Rāvaṇa's brother Khara, to protect spiritual practitioners and safeguard dharma, and urges Lakṣmaṇa to disfigure Rāvaṇa's sister Śūrpaṇakhā. In revenge, Rāvaṇa abducts Sītā from their hermitage, after his former minister Mārīca draws Rāma and Lakṣmaṇa away, and takes her to his capital Laṅkā. Rāma contracts an alliance with Sugrīva whom he installs as king of the monkeys by slaying his elder brother Vālin in exchange for Sugrīva's help in finding and recovering Sītā. He then marches on Laṅkā with Sugrīva and his army of monkeys and bears, accepts the allegiance of Rāvaṇa's younger brother Vibhīṣaṇa, defeats Rāvaṇa, installs Vibhīṣaṇa as king of Laṅkā, reunites with his wife Sītā and returns to Ayodhyā where his half-brother Bharata joyfully restores the kingdom to him.

2. The divine dimension

A divine dimension embraces the story of Rāma providing the impetus for the birth of Rāma, his brothers, and their companions and culminating in the achievement of the divine purpose. After he has been granted the boon by the creator god Brahmā that he be unslayable by gods, demons, and other classes of creatures, the Rākṣasa Rāvaṇa, wreaks havoc upon the three worlds. The gods and other righteous beings, unable to control him, approach Brahmā for help. Since Rāvaṇa neglected to include humans when he requested his boon, Viṣṇu incarnates in human form in order to slay him, and various classes of beings take birth, particularly as monkeys, in order to accompany him in the endeavor.

B. The *Rāmopākhyāna*

Consisting of about 25,000 verses in Vālmīki's *Rāmāyaṇa*, the story of Rāma was summarized in 704 verses in eighteen chapters in the *Rāmopākhyāna*, which comprises chapters 258–275 of the *Āraṇyaka Parvan* of the great epic *Mahābhārata.* The story is introduced in chapter 257, where king Yudhiṣṭhira, dejected over the recent abduction of his wife and the exile of his family to the forest, asks the sage Mārkaṇḍeya, "Have you seen or even heard of any man more unfortunate than I?" Mārkaṇḍeya uplifts Yudhiṣṭhira by telling him of Rāma, who, after similarly being exiled to the forest and having his wife abducted, eventually regained his kingdom. He concludes the story in chapter 276, where he encourages Yudhiṣṭhira to be resolute and not to despair (276.2) because he is virtuous (276.2) and great-souled (276.13), and he spells out the moral of the story in verses 4–12. "All aims attend upon the one who has companions" (276.5), he remonstrates after reminding Yudhiṣṭhira that Indra, the king of the gods, was victorious "by allying with the Maruts" (276.4). "Why do you despair," he asks, "with these companions" (276.7), pointing out Yudhiṣṭhira's mighty brothers who could conquer even Indra and the Maruts. Before recapitulating their recent recovery of their common wife Kṛṣṇā and their defeat of her abductor (276.9–10), he fortells, "You will conquer all enemies in battle with these god-like great archers as companions" (276.8). Finally, Mārkaṇḍeya concludes from the story just narrated in the *Rāmopākhyāna*, "With companions, Rāma slew Rāvaṇa in battle and recovered Sītā, having the monkeys and bears belonging to different species as his friends. Think about it!" (276.11–12). Yudhiṣṭhira then abandons his sorrow and in due time, after contracting many alliances, defeats his evil cousin in battle and recovers his kingdom.

C. Textual limits to the divine dimension

The divine dimension of the story acknowledges Rāma's humanity by necessitating Viṣṇu's incarnation in human form: Rāvaṇa can be slain only by a human due to the omission of the human (*ṛte manuṣyāt*) from the classes of creatures from whom Brahmā grants Rāvaṇa invincibility (259.26). However, while the divine dimension of the story of Rāma recognizes Rāma's humanity, it remains peripheral to the human story due to textual limitations of its narration and character limitations of its principal hero. Textually, the divine dimension of the story is not well intergrated into the narrative of Rāma either in the *Rāmāyaṇa* or in the *Rāmopākhyāna*. In both it is narrated in peripheral sections forming later additions to the text. Moreover, the narration of the story in response to Yudhiṣṭhira's question whether there is any man (*nara*) less fortunate than he (257.10) affirms Rāma's humanity and suggests that the story did not include its divine dimension when the *Rāmopākhyāna* was inserted into the *Mahābhārata*.

The divinity of the character of Rāma remains incompatible with his human shortcomings. Through the bulk of the story Rāma behaves as a human unaware of having the status of the supreme god Viṣṇu, as do his brothers, and Sītā betrays no knowledge of her status as Viṣṇu's consort Lakṣmī. Although the divine dimension of the story itself acknowledges Rāma's humanity, the human limitations Rāma displays in emotion, intelligence, and ethical judgement are irreconciliable with those expected of the supreme absolute, even incarnate in human form. Not only western scholars find them so. The literary tradition of the text itself reveals the dissatisfaction various redactors of the story have with these human limitations by the fact that they adapt the story to reconcile them with higher ideals. In the various versions of the story of Rāma in the long history of its retelling, redactors have infused their concerns into the altering narrative through their adaptations. Comparison of the various versions discloses which passages are adaptations. Investigating the nature of these adaptations reveals the concerns which inspired them, whether they be the adaptor's private concerns or those of their times and cultures, whether they be spiritual, psychological, social, or ethical.

1. Limits in the *Rāmāyaṇa*

In the *Rāmāyaṇa*, the incarnation of Viṣṇu as Daśaratha's sons and their reentrance into Viṣṇu's body are narrated in the first and final books. The presence of concluding verses and collophons, the mention of the recitation of the *Rāmāyaṇa* by Rāma's sons, and the participation of its author in its own *Bālakāṇḍa* and *Uttarakāṇḍa* signal that these are subsequent additions to the *Rāmāyaṇa*.[2] Three chapters interrupting the surrounding narrative in the *Bālakāṇḍa* (1.14–16) describe Rāvaṇa agitating the worlds, Viṣṇu taking birth as Daśaratha's four sons (1.14.18) at the request of the gods, and the gods following Viṣṇu in birth to be his companions. While Daśaratha is performing a rite to obtain sons, a divine man rises from the fire and gives rice-pudding to Daśaratha with instructions to feed it to his three wives (1.15.8–18). Daśaratha feeds half to Kausalyā, one quarter to Sumitrā, one eighth to Kaikeyī, and then the remaining eighth to Sumitrā (1.15.24–28). Three verses in the next chapter describe the portion of Viṣṇu in each son born. Kausalyā gives birth to Rāma as a half-portion of Viṣṇu, Kaikeyī to Bharata as a quarter portion, and Sumitrā to Lakṣmaṇa and Śatrughna, each as a half portion (1.17.6–9).[3] At the end of the *Uttarakāṇḍa*, when Lakṣmaṇa restrains his breath at the bank of the Sarayū river (15) and Indra brings him to heaven, the gods honor him as the fourth part of Viṣṇu (7.96.17–18), and when Rāma enters the Sarayū river with Bharata and Śatrughna followed by all his subjects, Brahmā welcomes Rāma and enjoins him to enter his own body of Viṣṇu with his brothers (7.100.6–10).

One chapter near the end of the *Yuddhakāṇḍa* (6.105) has the gods disclose the divine status of himself and Sītā to Rāma; yet in doing so it reaffirms their humanity and ignorance of their divine status throughout the narrative. When all the gods arrive upon Sītā's entrance into the fire after Rāma rejects her, they asks Rāma how he does not recognize

[2]See Brockington, *Righteous Rāma*.

[3]If the portions of Viṣṇu in each son corresponded to the proportions of rice-pudding in each portion the three wives ate, one would expect Rāma, Lakṣmaṇa, Bharata, and Śatrughna to be one half, one quarter, one eighth, and again one eighth portions of Viṣṇu respectively; moreover, Lakṣmaṇa is counted as a quarter portion of Viṣṇu upon his return. However, the mysteries of portions of the divine and of rice-pudding need not be constrained by arithmetic.

himself as the best of the host of gods (6.105.5). "For," they tell him, "you are the self-existent initial creator of the three worlds" (6.105.6) and reprimand him for disregarding Sītā "as if [he] were an ordinary human" (6.105.8). When Rāma answers that he considers himself to be human, Brahmā tells him that he is the immutable absolute (*brahman*), the supreme soul Viṣṇu, that Sītā is Lakṣmī, and that he entered human form to slay Rāvaṇa and bids him be content and return to heaven since the job has been done (6.105.10–27).

Besides this disclosure of Rāma's divine status, the *Yuddhakāṇḍa* refers to the divinity of the brothers only twice. The wise Rākṣasa Mālyavat, Rāvaṇa's maternal grandfather, tells Rāvaṇa that he considers Rāma to be Viṣṇu incarnate and advises him to make peace with him (6.26.31–32). Later Lakṣmaṇa remembers himself to be a portion of Viṣṇu when Rāvaṇa knocks him out by striking him between his breasts with Brahmā's weapon (6.47.104). Rāvaṇa is astonished seeing him as such when he is unable to budge him after trying to lift him in his arms (6.47.107). Lakṣmaṇa regains consciousness and is healed remembering himself as a portion of Viṣṇu (6.47.115).

In the bulk of the *Rāmāyaṇa*, however, no association is made between Rāma and Viṣṇu. In fact, such an association is explicitly denied. When Hanūmat is caught destroying the garden in Rāvaṇa's palace, Prahasta asks him whether he has been sent by Viṣṇu, among others (5.48.7). Hanūmat denies that he has (5.48.7), while affirming that he is a messenger of Rāma (5.48.16). Neither associates Viṣṇu with Rāma.

2. Limits in the *Rāmopākhyāna*

In the *Rāmopākhyāna*, the narration of the episodes of Rāvaṇa terrorizing the world and the birth of Viṣṇu and the other gods sits awkwardly in chapters 259–60. Mārkaṇḍeya answers Yudhiṣṭhira's initial query, whether he has seen anyone more miserable than he, in just three verses (258.1–3). Yudhiṣṭhira then poses several additional questions (258.4): first about Rāma's lineage, second about his might, third about Rāvaṇa's lineage, and fourth about the cause of the hostility between them. Then (258.5) he expresses his desire to hear about Rāma's deeds. Mārkaṇḍeya answers the first question in the next three verses (258.6–9), which make no mention of the incarnation of Viṣṇu. After a transitional sentence in which he promises to do so (258.10), he answers the third question in the next fourteen verses (258.11–259.8). The remainder of the chapter narrates how Rāvaṇa obtained his boon of invincibility from Brahmā and terrorized the worlds (259.9–40), and the next chapter (260) narrates the plea of the gods for help and the incarnation of Viṣṇu and the gods. In the verse immediately following (261.1), Yudhiṣṭhira acknowledges the narration of the birth of Rāma, etc. (*rāmādi*), and asks to hear how Rāma, Lakṣmaṇa, and Sītā were banished. He remains silent for the remainder of the story.

The narrative intervening between Yudhiṣṭhira's two interjections is excessive in addressing the third question about Rāvaṇa's lineage (14 verses in comparison to 3 verses in answer to the first question about Rāma's) and fails to answer the second and fourth questions, which remain unanswered until chapter 261. The narration of the episodes from Rāvaṇa's rise to power through the descent of Viṣṇu and the gods (259.9–260.15) neither answers Yudhiṣṭhira's previous questions nor meets his subsequent acknowledgement, because Yudhiṣṭhira has not previously learned of any connection between Viṣṇu and Rāma, and because it would be overly generous to stretch 'etc.' in 261.1 to include Viṣṇu and the gods when no question was posed about them.

The *Rāmopākhyāna* never explicitly identifies Rāma with Viṣṇu. While Brahmā mentions the incarnation of Viṣṇu in human form (260.5) and enjoins the gods to progenerate sons in bears and monkeys to be his companions (260.7), he does not specify the human form or forms in which he incarnates. Similarly, the *Rāmopākhyāna* does not include the reentrance of Rāma or his brothers into Viṣṇu's body. It ends with the return of Rāma, Sītā, and Lakṣmaṇa to Ayodhyā, followed by Rāma's coronation, and his performance of ten Aśvamedha Vedic performances. It does not include the contents of the *Uttarakāṇḍa*, a late addition to the *Rāmāyaṇa*, in which Rāma banishes Sītā when he learns of rumors criticizing him for accepting her back after she had been with another man. When all the gods arrive upon Rāma's initial rejection of her after Rāvaṇa's defeat, Brahmā tells Rāma that in slaying Rāvaṇa he has brought down an enemy of the gods (275.30) and carried out a great obligation for the gods (275.34). He even goes so far as to address him, "immortal-like one" (275.34), but he does not identify him with the absolute or with Viṣṇu. In fact, the only other mention of Viṣṇu in the *Rāmopākhyāna* is as the presiding deity of the constellation under which Rāma is consecrated king upon his return to Ayodhyā (275.65).

Mārkaṇḍeya's narration of the divine episodes in chapters 259–60 awkwardly interrupts his response to Yudhiṣṭhira's questions. His narration of the only other major divine episode, i.e. the appearance of the gods at Sītā's rejection, is confined to a single scene which is brought into question in our subsequent consideration of the ethical status of Rāma's action. The *Rāmopākhyāna* never assumes Rāma has the status of Viṣṇu, never, in fact, even identifying Rāma with Viṣṇu. Therefore, the narration of the story of Rāma in the *Rāmopākhyāna* would proceed smoothly without including the divine dimension at all.

D. Rāma and Sītā's humanity

1. Human emotions, intelligence, etc.

Throughout the *Rāmopākhyāna*, Rāma behaves very much as a human. He displays human emotions, human reasoning, human effort, and human vulnerability. He displays human emotions on numerous occasions. He sickens (*paryatapyata*) when he realizes that he has been drawn away from the hermitage by a Rākṣasa (262.12) and then rushes back with his heart burning (*dahyamānena ... hṛdā* 263.15). He and Lakṣmaṇa are "filled with sorrow and grief" (*duḥkhaśokasamāviṣṭa*) and "agitated" (*ardita*) when they set out in search of Sītā (263.23). When he and Lakṣmaṇa reach the river Pampā, he is "plunged in sorrow over the abduction of Sītā" (*sītāharaṇaduḥkhārta* 264.1). There he laments "pained (*abhisaṁtapta*) by the arrow of love" (264.3), and needs Lakṣmaṇa to help him regain his constitution. Lakṣmaṇa does so by reminding him, "This sort of emotion is not able to touch you." This is so not because he is divine, but rather because disease is unable to touch "a man (*puruṣa*) of healthy habits, possessed of the self" (264.4). Rāma is again "dispirited" (*durmanas*) remembering Sītā while staying atop Mount Mālyavat (266.4).

Rāma displays other human traits as well. He uses human reasoning to infer (*anumānena mene*) that Hanūmat has seen Sītā (266.29). Lakṣmaṇa explicitly urges Rāma to rescue Sītā "by human effort and intelligence" (*puruṣakāreṇa buddhyā ca*) (264.5). Rāma needs to be told by Lakṣmaṇa to slay the images of himself which Rāvaṇa makes (274.11) and needs to be reassured by Vibhīṣaṇa that Mātali is not a fake (274.15). Defeated (272.26) and bound with arrows (373.1) by Indrajit, Rāma and Lakṣmaṇa, are brought back to consciousness by Vibhīṣaṇa and healed by Sugrīva (273.5–7). Sītā too behaves as a human. She, in fact, explicitly refers to her own humanity when she tells Rāvaṇa, in answer to his request for her to marry him, that "a pitiable human wife (*bhāryā mānuṣī kr̥paṇā*)" would not be suitable for him (265.21).

2. Rāma's ethics

The ethical propriety of some of Rāma's actions is less than ideal. Three deeds in particular deserve censure: his telling Lakṣmaṇa to mutilate Śūrpaṇakhā, his slaying of Vālin, and his rejection of Sītā.

a. The mutilation of Śūrpaṇakhā

The *Rāmopākhyāna* narrates only that Śūrpaṇakhā brought about hostilities between Rāma and Rāvaṇa's brother Khara, that Rāma slew Khara and Dūṣaṇa, and that Śūrpaṇakhā, whose nose and lips had been cut, sought refuge with her brother Rāvaṇa in Laṅkā (261.41–45). The *Rāmāyaṇa*, however, supplies details of how Śūrpaṇakhā brought about hostilities, and it implicates Rāma himself as responsible. Śūrpaṇakhā approaches Rāma sitting telling stories with Lakṣmaṇa and Sītā. When she proposes to marry him and to eat Lakṣmaṇa and Sītā, Rāma jokingly demurs on the grounds that she wouldn't enjoy being a co-wife to Sītā. He suggests rather that she take the unmarried Lakṣmaṇa who wants a wife. When Śūrpaṇakhā proposes to Lakṣmaṇa, he too jokingly demurs. His grounds are that she would be happier as the younger co-wife of Rāma, of whom he is merely the servant and who would abandon his old, ugly wife for her. Śūrpaṇakhā, not comprehending that Rāma and Lakṣmaṇa are toying with her, again proposes to marry Rama and to eat Sītā. When she suddenly rushes towards Sītā, Rāma reproves Lakṣmaṇa for (merely) joking with cruel ignobles (*anārya* 'non-Aryan') and tells him to mutilate Śūrpaṇakhā, whereupon Lakṣmaṇa cuts off her ears and nose (*R.* 3.16.21–17.21).

Rāma's nasty toying with Śūrpaṇakhā and his bidding Lakṣmaṇa to mutilate her lead directly to war with her brother Khara and prompt

Rāvaṇa to take revenge by abducting Sītā. While Rāma cannot be held responsible for the excessive countermeasures of her relatives, he certainly provoked them and regardless of them must be held responsible for his own injudicious excesses against Śūrpaṇakhā.

b. The slaying of Vālin

According to the terms of his treaty with Sugrīva (264.11–14, 21), Rāma slays Sugrīva's elder brother Vālin and installs Sugrīva as king in Kiṣkindhā in exchange for his help in finding and recovering Sītā. He slays Vālin by shooting him with an arrow from hiding while Vālin is engaged in one-on-one combat with Sugrīva. The texts themselves censure Rāma's foul deed by the fact that the dying victim rebukes him for it (264.35–38). While it may be true that Vālin transgressed against Sugrīva by banishing him from the kingdom, taking his wife Rumā, imprisoning his friends, and attempting to assassinate him (*R.* 4.8.31–33, 4.10.21–22), these excesses originated from grounded suspicions. When he overcame the demon Māyāvin in his cave, instead of finding Sugrīva at the mouth of the cave where he had asked him to remain guard, he found the mouth of the cave blocked and Sugrīva sitting in his place on the throne. Although Vālin had rejected Sugrīva's explanations, apologies, and gestures to return the kingdom and serve his brother again as he had previously (*R.* 4.10.1–7), Rāma himself makes no effort at conciliation and hears no testimony from Vālin. He simply passes judgement (*kr̥takilbiṣa R.* 4.8.23) and assasinates him for taking Sugrīva's wife (*bhāryāpahārin R.* 4.8.20, *R.* 4.10.28) even though Sugrīva had taken his wife Tārā after blocking the mouth of the cave and assuming the throne in Kiṣkindhā (*R.* 4.45.8, 4.54.3).[4]

c. The rejection of Sītā

In the *Rāmopākhyāna*, when the aged Rākṣasa Avindhya presents Sītā to him after Rāvaṇa's defeat (275.6–7), Rāma initially rejects her. He tells her he has done his duty in liberating her from Rāvaṇa and bids her to go because a man resolute in dharma cannot support a woman who has been in another man's arms and because he will not be able to enjoy her now that she has been polluted, even if her own conduct was

[4]See Tārā, Rāma, Vālin, and Sugrīva in the A, 264.11–39, and *R.* 4.8.16–4.10.23. Matilal (1982), however, argues that Rāma's deed formally accords with dharma.

good (275.10–13). He accepts her (275.38) only after Brahmā, Vāyu, Agni, Varuṇa, and his deceased father vouch for her purity and urge him to do so (275.17–35). Vāyu testifies that she is sinless (275.26), Agni that she has "not gone astray even very minutely" (275.27), and Brahmā that Rāvaṇa couldn't have raped her because his body would have burst into a hundred pieces due to the curse of Nalakūbara, whose bride he had raped previously (275.32–34).

In the *Rāmāyaṇa*, Rāma accepts her again only after Agni, the fire which she enters in order to prove her devotion, restores her to him (*R.* 6.106.3–20). After their return to Ayodhyā, however, he commands Lakṣmaṇa (*R.* 7.44.15–17) to take her to the other side of the Ganges near Valmīki's hermitage and to abandon her (*R.* 7.46.13–15, 7.47.14–15) out of his concern for public opinion (*R.* 7.87.14–15, 20, *R.* 7.88.3) because of complaints about the example he set by accepting her back (*R.* 7.42.16–19).

That he should cast off the innocent victim of abduction out of his or the public's unsubstantiated suspicion of her abductor's physical violation of her certainly offends contemporary western ethical sensibilities. But beyond cultural prejudice, internal literary evidence reveals that it offends ancient Indian sensibilities as well. Characters in both the *Rāmopākhyāna* and the *Rāmāyaṇa* express their disapproval. In response to his rejection of her in the *Rāmopākhyāna*, the monkeys become motionless and their breaths become still (275.16), and Brahmā, a whole host of gods, and Rāma's father appear to object (275.17–20).

Similarly, when Sītā enters the fire at the end of the *Yuddhakāṇḍa* in the *Rāmāyaṇa*, the gods Vaiśravaṇa, Yama, Indra, Varuṇa, Śiva, and Brahmā arrive. Addressing Rāma as the creator of the whole world and best of the wise, they question his indifference to Sītā falling into the flames (*R.* 6.105.5) and scold him for being indifferent to her like an ordinary man (*R.* 6.105.8). The text describes Rāma's speech rejecting Sītā as harsh (*paruṣa R.* 6.103.12, 104.1, *rūkṣa R.* 6.104.2). In her response, Sītā herself criticizes Rāma for addressing her "as a common man addresses an ordinary woman" (*R.* 6.104.5) and for prejudicial judgement against her as a woman. She asks him to judge her by her own behavior in her vow to him rather than suspecting womankind (*strīṇām . . . jāti, strītva*) generically by prevalent behavior (*R.* 6.104.6–7). She faults him for setting womankind generically before himself like a worthless man and ignoring her devotion and good conduct, rather than making the specifics of her behavior, which are well known to him, the standard of his judgement (*R.* 6.104.14–16). In the *Uttarakāṇḍa*, Lakṣmaṇa is tormented while carrying out Rāma's command to abandon Sītā and tells her, "You have been abandoned by the king fearful of the criticism of his citizens even though you are faultless in my view" (*R.* 7.46.13).

The fact that Rāma ultimately seeks reconciliation with Sītā after their sons sing the *Rāmāyaṇa* to him at his performance of an Aśvamedha Vedic ceremony (*R.* 7.86.4–6, *R.* 7.88.4) testifies to the *Uttarakāṇḍa*'s discomfort with his banishing her. Vālmīki presents Sītā to him before the whole world, which gathers to witness her swear another oath. Describing her as impeccable, dharma-practicing, of pure conduct, true to her vows, and devoted to her husband, he says, "she will give proof to you who are fearful of public criticism" (*R.* 7.87.14–15). Rāma himself, acknowledging that she had previously given proof in the presence of the gods, answers, "Sītā was abandoned by me, even though I knew that she was sinless, out of fear of the public." After asking Vālmīki for forgiveness (*tad bhavān kṣantum arhasi R.* 7.88.3), he says, "Let me be pleased with the pure princess of Mithilā in the midst of the whole world" (*R.* 7.88.4). Sītā gives the second proof of her fidelity but denies Rāma a second chance. With a nod from Vālmīki, she swears, "If I never even think of anyone other than Rāma with my mind let the goddess Earth open to receive me." At once, a supreme, gem-studded celestial throne rises out of the earth on the heads of powerful serpents, the goddess Earth takes Sītā in her arms, seats her on it, and descends into the earth again (7.88.10–14).

E. Moral versus mundane factors in Sītā's rejection

Close analysis of the arguments defending Sītā and justifying Rāma's rejection of her reveal a distinction between internal and external factors, both in the *Rāmāyaṇa* and in the *Rāmopākhyāna*. Internal factors such as Rāma's suspicion and Sītā's fidelity are distinguished from and set in opposition to external factors such as public opinion and physical impurity. This distinction is apparent despite being blurred by the incongruency of charges and replies, answering an external charge with an internal defense and vice versa. While Rāma indicts Sītā for physical impurity, her defense denies her complicity rather than her pollution. While her defense attests to her pure intentions and conduct, justifications of Rāma's rejection of her point to public opinion.

The incongruity of Sītā's defense with Rāma's accusations is particularly pointed in the *Rāmopākhyāna*. Although Rāma rejects Sītā, regardless of her conduct, because she has been in another man's arms and is polluted, Sītā, Vāyu, and Agni defend the purity of her conduct rather than the purity of her body. She asks the wind and the elements to release her life breaths if she has sinned (*pāpaṁ carāmi*), and Vāyu and Agni assert that she is sinless (*apāpa*) and has not gone astray (*nāparādhyati*). Even Brahmā's testimony, which does certify her physical purity, is incongruent with the charges. The certification of her physical purity is valid only under the assumption that her intentions were pure. Nalakūbara's curse protects a woman from Rāvaṇa's touch only if she is unwilling (*akāma*), not if she is willing.

In the *Rāmāyaṇa*, Rāma raises doubts both about Sītā's conduct (*R.* 6.103.17) and about her physical purity. He raises the issue of physical violation by inferring that Rāvaṇa has violated her and by questioning the possibility of receiving her again. He asks, "How could I, representing a great family, take you back after you have fallen into Rāvaṇa's lap and been beheld by his filthy vision?" (*R.* 6.103.20). The question assumes his inference, "For Rāvaṇa is not going to allow you moving about in his own house to disregard him for long after beholding you, divinely beautiful and pleasing, Sītā (6.103.24)."

Incongruently in reply, Sītā does not deny physical violation; she denies only misconduct and infidelity. She admits that her body came into contact with another but argues that it was against her will and beyond her control, that it was fate that transgressed, not she (*R.* 6.104.8). "What is under my control, my heart," she says, "is devoted to you" (*R.* 6.104.9). She then undertakes the fire ordeal to prove her fidelity, not to incinerate the pollution of Rāvaṇa's touch. She enters the flames asking Agni to grant her protection, "as my heart has never left Rāma" (*R.* 6.104.25). Agni restores her to Rāma, thereby certifying her good conduct and fidelity, not her physical purity (*R.* 6.106.1–9). He testifies that she did not transgress, is sinless in speech, mind, memory, and glance, was taken against her will, is of pure emotion, is completely devoted to and always thinking of Rāma, and never gave place to a single thought for Rāvaṇa (*R.* 6.106.4–9).

Despite the fact that the distinction between internal and external factors is blurred by the incongruency of charges and replies, it is evident that Rāma's rejection of Sītā is founded upon the external factors of her having been polluted by Rāvaṇa's touch and his concern for public opinion, while the internal factor, her fidelity, is diminished and even denied. After Agni vouches for Sītā's fidelity, Rāma denies that he ever doubted it. He asserts that he knows Sītā keeps her thoughts on him, is devoted to him, and has only him in her heart (*R.* 6.106.13). He disregarded Sītā entering the fire, he parries, "for the sake of proving it to the three worlds" (*R.* 6.106.14).

The external factors adduced as grounds for Sītā's initial rejection in Laṅkā and for her subsequent banishment as narrated in the *Uttarakāṇḍa*, however, are insufficient grounds for the indictments and punishments for which they are adduced. If Rāvaṇa's touch rather than Sītā's infidelity is the reason for rejecting her, then why doesn't Rāma reject Lakṣmaṇa whom Rāvaṇa has taken in his arms (§IC1, *R.* 6.47.107)? If the case is distinguished when it concerns a man's wife, why doesn't he reject Sītā after rescuing her from Virādha who abducts her prior to Rāvaṇa in the *Araṇyakāṇḍa* of the *Rāmāyaṇa* (*R.* 3.2–3)? Why doesn't Yudhiṣṭhira reject Kṛṣṇā after slaying her abductor Jayadratha? One could argue for distinguishing Sītā's case from the latter two on the grounds that they are brief while Sītā dwells in Rāvaṇa's house for several months. Rāma does ask when initially rejecting Sītā, "What man born in a noble family would take back a woman who has dwelt in another man's house?" (*R.* 6.103.19). But how long does it take? If Yudhiṣṭhira could accept Kṛṣṇā back and Rāma could accept Sītā back after Virādha's abduction, why can't he accept her back after defeating Rāvaṇa? If physical impurity is not the reason for rejecting Sītā, why is it adduced? Why isn't suspicion of Sītā's infidelity a good reason?

If Rāma does truly believe in Sītā's fidelity, his rejecting her in Laṅkā and subsequently banishing her can only have to do with public opinion. His rejection of her in Laṅkā gives her the opportunity to prove her innocence to the armies of monkeys and bears and Rākṣasas, or, more generously as he claims, to the three worlds. But if her innocence has been proven to the three worlds in Laṅkā, how can public criticism of his accepting her back arise subsequently, and why is this criticism accepted as legitimate grounds for her banishment? Is the demonstration of her fidelity in Laṅkā unacceptable evidence for the citizens of Ayodhyā that they require a second? If so, why not offer her the opportunity to prove her innocence right away by publicly rejecting her immediately, rather than commanding Lakṣmaṇa to escort her quietly to the edge of the kingdom to abandon her to live in sorrow divorced from her husband until her children grow up? If public censure is grounds for banishing her because accepting back one's wife after she has dwelt in another man's house sets a bad example for the populace (*R.* 7.42.16–19), what kind of example does it set to punish the innocent victim of abduction on the grounds of unsubstantiated suspicion of her impurity or infidelity?

F. Moral revisionism in narrative adaptation

If the external factors adduced as grounds for Sītā's initial rejection and subsequent banishment are insufficient to justify Rāma's actions, one can only accept that what motivates him is suspicion of Sītā's infidelity. If that is so, why are Rāma's accusations incongruent with Sītā's defense? In particular, why do both the *Rāmopākhyāna* and the *Rāmāyaṇa* dislocate the charges against Sītā from the realm of her heart to the realm of her body and from the realm of Rāma's suspicion to that of his reputation? The transfer of Rāma's accusations from internal factors to external factors must be recognized as a mechanism of redactors to defend Rāma against criticism that he punished Sītā undeservedly.

If what is at issue is Sītā's fidelity, i.e. the disposition of her heart and will, any punishment meted out to her is a punishment of her infidelity, her intentional misconduct. Rāma is the agent of this punishment in his rebuttal of her at Laṅkā and in his subsequent banishment of her from Ayodhyā. Hence Rāma's punishment of Sītā is pitted directly against Sītā's inner disposition, and the assertion of Sītā's innocence and fidelity is therefore an implicit criticism of Rāma's rejection of her. The opposition between Rāma's rejection of Sītā and the undeservability of Sītā's punishment must shift into other realms if both the impeccability of Rāma's behavior and Sītā's fidelity are to be preserved.

It becomes more imperative to remove the opposition from their inner selves as Rāma and Sītā's status is raised from that of ordinary human beings to exemplars of human conduct and ultimately to the self-conscious incarnations of omniscient, compassionate deities. Subsequent redactions of the story of Rāma have altered the narrative in response to psychological discomfort with Sītā's pollution and ethical discomfort with Rāma's rejection of her in earlier narratives. Rāmānanda in his *Adhyātmarāmāyaṇa* (14th c.) and Tulasīdāsa in his *Rāmacaritamānasa* (1574–77), for example, adopt the device of the shadow Sītā to remove the stain of Rāvaṇa's touch completely from the real Sītā, to shield her from the sorrow and humiliation of Rāma's rejection, and to relieve Rāma of the role of her unjust and incompassionate accuser. Rāvaṇa abducts the shadow Sītā, whom Rāma rejects and the fire consumes before it returns the real Sītā, unsullied, to her husband. Thereby the fully self-conscious incarnations of Viṣṇu and Lakṣmī remain impeccable both mentally and physically.[5]

Conversely, the trend of adapting the text to defend their behavior as Rāma and Sītā become associated with Viṣṇu and Lakṣmī and elevated to divine status begins before the finalization of the extant versions of the *Rāmāyaṇa* and *Rāmopākhyāna*. The textual factors discussed in §IC disclose that these texts incorporate adaptations to earlier versions of the story. It is very probable that earlier versions of the story of Rāma excluded, not only the subject matter of the *Bālakāṇḍa* and *Uttarakāṇḍa* of the *Rāmāyaṇa*, but also the entire episode of Rāma's rejection of Sītā, her ordeal to prove her purity, and the arrival of the gods. It is even likely that versions of the *Rāmopākhyāna* of the *Mahābhārata* and the *Yuddhakāṇḍa* of the *Rāmāyaṇa* themselves circulated without these episodes.

[5]I treat the topic more fully in my paper, "Public and private ethics." Hess, "Rejecting Sita," observes Tulasīdās's double parry (pp. 9–10) and Sagar's contemporary televised variation of it (pp. 11–14). She also documents recent retellings of the fire ordeal censuring Rāma's rejection of Sītā.

1. Parallels to Sītā's case

In the *Mahābhārata*, in sharp contrast to Rāma's rejection of Sītā, Yudhiṣṭhira is neither suspicious of Kṛṣṇā's complicity nor anxious about her impurity. He expresses only concern that she has suffered. Moreover, his concern for her suffering even exceeds his sorrow over the loss of his kingdom and the exile of himself and his brothers to the forest. Just after Mārkaṇḍeya has comforted him with the story of Rāma's recovery of his wife and kingdom, Yudhiṣṭhira remarks (277.1), "I don't grieve for myself or for my brothers or for the seizing of the kingdom as much as for the daughter of Drupada (Kṛṣṇā)." He regrets Kṛṣṇā's abduction more than the loss of his kingdom even after her recovery. Far from questioning her fidelity, he promptly asks Mārkaṇḍeya whether he has seen or heard of any wife more devoted to her husband than Kṛṣṇā (277.3).

Ironically, Mārkaṇḍeya commences the tale of Sāvitrī as the paradigm of devotion to her husband rather than referring back to Sītā. Even after hearing how Sītā left a trail for her rescuers by dropping her ornaments and garments and remained unwaveringly devoted to Rāma for months in captivity while Rāvaṇa pleaded with her to become his chief queen, it does not occur to Yudhiṣṭhira that she is comparable to his own wife Kṛṣṇā, who saved him and his brothers when they were afflicted by their rogue cousin and his uncle in the dice-match (277.2). Kṛṣṇā's resourcefulness entitles her to be compared with Sāvitrī who single-handedly saved her husband from death, restored vision to her father-in-law, and obtained sons for her father.

Rāma himself raises no suspicion of Sītā's complicity and no concern with her impurity in the episode of her abduction by Virādha in the *Rāmāyaṇa*. Similar to Yudhiṣṭhira's superlative concern for Kṛṣṇā, he expresses only concern for Sītā's suffering, greater than for the death of his father and loss of his kingdom (*R.* 3.2.19). In an earlier version of the story of Rāma, Rāma probably does accept Sītā back without question just as Yudhiṣṭhira accepts Kṛṣṇā and just as Rāma himself accepts Sītā in the Virādha episode. Rāma's rejection and Sītā's ordeal were added subsequently, reflecting psychological discomfort with the pollution of one's wife sullied by another man, as well as social concern for sexual promiscuity and the purity of the family line.

2. Comparison of Yudhiṣṭhira's and Rāma's exiles

Rāma's circumstances are similar to Yudhiṣṭhira's in several other respects besides the abduction of his wife. He is exiled to the forest because of his step-mother's greed for her son to rule the kingdom, as Yudhiṣṭhira is because of his cousin Duryodhana's greed to rule. He is accompanied by his wife Sītā and his brother Lakṣmaṇa, as Yudhiṣṭhira is by his wife Kṛṣṇā and his five brothers. He recovers his abducted wife and his kingdom, as does Yudhiṣṭhira. Despite these similarities, however, it is remarkable how sharply the conditions of his departure and return to his kingdom contrast with Yudhiṣṭhira's. Rāma's departure is characterized by peaceful adherence to truth as opposed to bitter resentment, and his return by devotion and joy as opposed to strife and sorrow.

Yudhiṣṭhira is forced to reside in the forest for twelve years and to remain hidden for a thirteenth by the wager he agrees to in a dice match. His cousin Duryodhana, who has long been scheming to acquire control of his share of the kingdom, defeats him in the match by cheating and refuses to return the kingdom to him when he claims it thirteen years later. Yudhiṣṭhira recovers it only after a prolonged war.

In contrast, Rāma departs for the forest voluntarily in order that his father remain true to the promise he made to his second wife Kaikeyī, even though that promise puts her son Bharata on the throne in his stead. Bharata, far from scheming to acquire the kingdom from his elder half brother, is absent when his mother makes the request on his behalf. Far from refusing to hand over the kingdom upon Rāma's return, Bharata renounces the crown and sets out to bring Rāma back, rules the kingdom in Rāma's name when Rāma insists on remaining in the forest, and joyfully relinquishes the kingdom when he finally does return. The mutual devotion of Rāma and his brothers, their abhorrence of self-aggrandizement, and their unhesitating adherence to truth and right, regardless of the personal consequences, sets them apart as exemplary standards of virtue. Bharata, in particular, displays the epitome of morality, unhesitantly dismissing the riches and power of the kingdom out of devotion to his brother.

The contrast between Rāma's relation with his brothers and Yudhiṣṭhira's with his cousins is so striking that it suggests that the story of Rāma, including the exemplary brotherly warmth, was deliberately composed as a moral critique of the *Mahābhārata*. Conversely, a simpler, less ideal story of Rāma may have preceded the composition of a redaction which serves as a moral critique of the *Mahābhārata*. With great distress at stripping it of its most noble and endearing characteristics, one can imagine the story of Rāma pervaded with more ordinary human motivations as a realistic narrative of historical events.

G. The historical basis

It is plausible that the story of Rāma is based upon an historical event. Sanskrit and Vedic culture were gradually spreading southward in the first millennium BC as was the political and military influence of the Sanskrit-speaking people inhabiting northern India. It is therefore plausible that a northern prince like Rāma, deprived of inheriting the throne in his own kingdom (as Rāma was by the machinations of his step-mother Kaikeyī), traveled southward, contracted an alliance with the disenfranchised younger brother of a neutral southern king (as Rāma did with Vālin's banished younger brother Sugrīva), slew his brother and seated him on the throne, marched against a hostile king on the island of Śrīlaṅkā with the support of his new ally (as Rāma did against Rāvaṇa), accepted the allegiance of the hostile king's younger brother, defeated the hostile king and seated the friendly younger brother on the throne (as Rāma did Vibhīṣaṇa), then returned to his own kingdom accompanied by the two allies he had won, and acceded to the throne of which he had been deprived.

The narration of such a story to Yudhiṣṭhira, unjustly deprived of his kingdom, would make a most fitting lesson for him at the place where the *Rāmopākhyāna* occurs in the *Mahābhārata*.

1. The monkeys

It would be unrealistic to accept as an historical basis for the story of Rāma that an exiled king formed an alliance with a kingdom of monkeys. However, few of the terms used to refer to the monkeys who help Rāma conquer Laṅkā in the *Rāmāyaṇa* and *Rāmopākhyāna* necessarily denote the animal. The most frequent of them probably denoted people of different ethnicity.

In the *Rāmopākhyāna*, by far the commonest term used to refer to the monkeys is *vānara*, occurring more frequently than any of the other terms put together (57x). The term *vā-nara* is a karmadhāraya compound formed from the particle *vā* 'or' and the noun *nara* 'man,' similar in formation to the compounds *kim-puruṣa* and *kim-nara*. The latter compounds, as derived from the interrogative pronoun *kim* 'what' and the nouns *puruṣa* or *nara* 'man' in accordance with *A.* 2.1.64, mean a questionable sort of man in a derogatory sense. While related words like *kāpuruṣa* refer to base men, the terms *kiṁpuruṣa* and *kiṁnara* in mythology refer to classes of beings associated with the atmospheric deities called Gandharvas, and the *Rāmāyaṇa* relates a story of their origin from men turned into women (*R.* 7.79). Since the terms refer derogatorily to men derivationally and apply to classes of beings mythologically, it seems reasonable to infer that they refer to peoples of different ethnicity historically. The analogously formed compound *vā-nara* therefore must originally have had a similar sense and referred to peoples of different ethnic origins.

Three of the other terms for the monkeys refer primarily to color and gait rather than to species. The term *hari* (27x) refers, in addition to monkeys, more often to horses, and also to lions, the sun, the moon, and many other things, deriving these designations from its use as an adjective for things of the color yellow which it primarily denotes (though it is also derivable as an agent noun from the verbal root √*hṛ* 'take, carry'). The terms *plava-ga* (8x) and *plavaṁ-gama* (2x) denote agents who go by leaping and may refer to the flickering fire, deer, and frogs as well as to monkeys. Even the term *kapi* (19x), which primarily denotes an ape or monkey, is derived from the verbal root √*kap* 'move, tremble' and could denote anything that moves, including an elephant and the Sun.

Two verses (267.8, 11) seem to describe smearing paste on the face, a practice of peoples rather than of monkeys, supporting the view that the bears mentioned in Sugrīva's army are people of a certain religious sect rather than animals. Commenting upon 267.8, Nīlakaṇṭha interprets the streaks on the faces of the bears led by Jāmbavat as sectarian marks. Similarly, though it may be an analogy rather than a description, 267.11 characterizes the monkeys as having vermilion-paste on their faces.

It is plausible that in an historical basis of the story of Rāma an exiled king forms an alliance with peoples of different ethnicity to help him recover his kingdom. Mārkaṇḍeya may, in fact, advise Yudhiṣṭhira to do just this when he concludes from his narration of the *Rāmopākhyāna* that Rāma slew Rāvaṇa and recovered Sītā with friends of different genera (§IB, 276.11–12).

H. The spiritual dimension

There is more to literature than history. Although the story of Rāma may be based upon historical events, its broad and lasting appeal is due to the rich fabric of mythological, moral, and spiritual elements which it comprises. The spiritual dimension pervading the story appears on the surface in the vast array of mythological characters which make their entrance into the story, in the magical powers and weapons employed, in the references to sages and spiritual practice, and most of all in the divine dimension of the incarnation of Viṣṇu. Although these elements take on popular characterizations in the narration of the story of Rāma, they remain metaphorical and direct indicators of profound spiritual understanding inherent in the Vedic tradition of India.

1. Various classes of beings

Besides humans and monkeys, the various classes of creatures entering into the story include gods (*deva*, *sura*); atmospheric divinities including Gandharvas, Cāraṇas, Yakṣas, and Apsarases; Kiṁnaras (called also *kiṁpuruṣa*); serpents (*sarpa*, *bhogin*, *pannaga*); ghosts (*bhūta*), and various classes of demons (*asura*) including Dānavas, Daityas, Piśācas, and Rākṣasas (called also *rakṣas*). Classes of sages include great sages (*maharṣi*), Brahman sages (*brahmarṣi*), royal sages (*rājarṣi*), the seven seers (*saptarṣi*), and the perfected ones (*siddha*). Many classes include both males and females, though Apsarases are specifically female. The Gandharvas include the female Dundubhī (260.9), the Rākṣasas the water-demoness whom Hanūmat slays (266.57), and Sītā's female guards. Rāvaṇa has women of the gods, royal-sages (*rājarṣi*), Dānavas, and Daityas. Rākṣasas, called night-rangers, man-eaters and flesh-eaters, include Rāvaṇa, his family, ministers, and soldiers but are not all bad. Many Rākṣasas, for instance, flee Laṅkā with Vaiśravaṇa when Rāvaṇa ousts him (259.33), and Vaiśravaṇa gives the virtuous

Rākṣasa Vibhīṣaṇa command over both the armies of Yakṣas and Rākṣasas (259.37). Piśācas, often indistinguishable from Rākṣasas, are not necessarily bad either. Sītā's guards, listed by name and called both *rākṣasī* and *piśācī* (264.43, 264.46, 264.73), include Sītā's comforter Trijaṭā.

2. Siddhis

Rākṣasas are often described as having special powers. Rāvaṇa and Kumbhakarṇa are described as "possessing special powers" (*māyāvin* 274.5, 259.11) and Indrajit as possessing many special powers (*bahumāya* 272.20). Rāvaṇa takes Sītā through the atmosphere (*vihāyasā*) by resorting to special power (*māyām āsthāya* 258.2). He effects his special power (*māyām ... vyadadhāt* 274.5, 7) by emitting Rākṣasas (274.6) and weapons (274.21–23) from his body and by creating likenesses of Rāma and Lakṣmaṇa (274.8–10). Indrajit turns invisible (*antar√dhā*) by special power (*māyā* 272.19, 22) and when invisible (*adr̥śya*) is described as hidden by special power (*māyayā vr̥taḥ* 272.25). Such an ability is described by *Yogasūtra* 3.21.

Although the term *māyā* is interpreted to mean illusion in Vedānta philosophy and is popularly etymologized to mean 'that which is not' from the prohibitive particle *mā* and the feminine nominative singular relative pronoun *yā*, it need not have a negative sense. In earlier Sanskrit it means 'art, wisdom, extraordinary power' and it is correctly derived from the verbal root √*mā* 'measure, make.'

The *Rāmopākhyāna* describes special powers even without using the term *māyā*. Other Rākṣasas have them. Rāvaṇa's former minister Mārīca takes the form of a bejeweled deer to entice Sītā into sending Rāma after him (262.11, 17). A number of other Rākṣasas become invisible and attack the monkeys while they are resting (269.1–3).

The Rākṣasa Vibhīṣaṇa is able to see through these special powers and to destroy them. He strikes down the invisibility of the Rākṣasas attacking the monkeys resting. (269.3) He reassures Rāma that the appearance of Indra's charioteer and chariot is genuine when Rāma suspects that it has appeared by Rāvaṇa's special power (*māyā* 274.15–16).

Although the *Rāmopākhyāna* reserves the term *māyā* for the special powers of Rākṣasas, monkeys have some special abilities too. Hanūmat seems to have the ability to fly and to grow large in size. He enters the wind and floats across the straits to Laṅkā (266.57) afterwards telling Sītā, "I have come here through the air" (266.60), and he slays Dhūmrākṣa "with his enormous body" (270.14). Searching for Indrajit when he has turned invisible, the monkeys are said to "enter the sky" (272.24).

When Saṁpāti tells the monkeys searching the South that he has seen Sītā in Rāvaṇa's city on the other side of the ocean, Hanūmat reports, they "stood up quickly and did a mantra (*mantraṁ mantrayāmaḥ*) for floating over the ocean" (*sāgaraplavane* 266.56). In the text this is translated, "stood up quickly and consulted about a plan for leaping over the ocean," because the verb √*mantr* often means simply 'consult' or 'plan,' and *mantra* often means simply 'counsel.' For example, √*mantr* means 'consult' when Daśaratha consults with his ministers (261.7), who are ordinarily called *mantrin* 'possessing mantras' (261.8), and means 'plan,' when Rāvaṇa and Mārīca carry out what they have planned previously (262.15). Similarly, the term *mantrānucara* 'one who attends another with sacred formulas' refers simply to a counselor (267.49). This type of consultation is precisely what Rāma undertakes with the monkey-leaders when he arrives at the straits of Laṅkā with the army of monkeys (267.24–29) in the directly comparable situation.

However, the verb √*mantr* also means to recite a Vedic formula called a *mantra*. In the *Rāmopākhyāna* the verb √*mantr* with the preverb *abhi* or *prati* is used to refer to the consecration of weapons by uttering formulas over them. Vibhīṣaṇa consecrates (*abhimantrya*) a missile he throws at Prahasta's head (270.3). Rāma threatens to use weapons consecrated with divine missiles (*divyāstrapratimantrita*) to coerce the ocean into letting his army pass (267.37), and he yokes (274.24) or consecrates (274.25) a golden shaft with Brahmā's weapon to bring Rāvaṇa to his end. Since Brahmā's weapon is referred to as 'that with which the shaft is consecrated' (*abhimantrita*), Brahmā's weapon refers to the sacred formula recited over the golden shaft. As a formula, it is something to be learned. Hence it makes sense that Vibhīṣaṇa requests as his boon from Brahmā that the weapon appear to him untaught (259.30). Lakṣmaṇa uses the same weapon, called also there a *divyāstra* 'divine weapon,' to bring an end to Kumbhakarṇa (271.16–17), and both he and Indrajit are referred to as 'knowing divine weapons' (272.11). The term *mantra* is used not only for formulas to unleash divine weapons but also for formulas accompanying the application of medicinal herbs (273.6).

Because the term *mantra* is used in the sense of a sacred formula and the verb √*mantr* in the sense of employing such a formula, Hanūmat's description of the monkeys standing up and doing a mantra (*mantraṁ mantrayāmaḥ*) for floating over the ocean (*sāgaraplavane* 266.56) could be interpreted to mean that they undertook a group performance to bring about the special ability to fly over the ocean, an ability which only Hanūmat was able to achieve (266.57). *Yogasūtra* 3.42 describes the ability to fly arising from the use of such a formula.

Besides Hanūmat, the monkey-leader Nala has a special ability: the ability to make anything float. He constructs a floating causeway from Rāmeśvara to Śrīlaṅkā for the army of monkeys to pass as the ocean promised Rāma in a dream that he would support whatever Nala threw in him (3.267.41–45). Rāma, Lakṣmaṇa, the king of the bears Jāmbavat, and a number of monkey-leaders gain the ability to see invisible Rākṣasas by applying a certain water sent by Vaiśravaṇa from the White Mountain (3.273.9–14).

The ability to see invisible creatures is an ability extraordinary for humans and animals, but its bestowal upon Rāma and the others by means of the application of a special fluid to the eyes is treated in the text comparably to the use of healing powers and medicinal herbs. In the same scene, just prior to presenting the Guhyaka who has brought the special water, Vibhīṣaṇa restores Rāma and Lakṣmaṇa to consciousness with the 'missile of consciousness' (*prajñāstra*) and Sugrīva instantly frees them from arrows with the great medicinal herb Viśalyā employed with sacred formulas (*divyamantra* 273.5–7). The text treats the abilities to restore consciousness, heal wounds, and bestow clairvoyance equally as technical methodologies, the latter two utilizing specialized substances: an herb and water.

The text does not describe the missile of consciousness Vibhīṣaṇa employs. But given the nature of what it accomplishes, rather than assume it is a physical substance as missiles (*astra*) ordinarily are, compare it with Brahmā's weapon (*brahmāstra*). The latter is a sacred formula to be recited. The term *brahmāstra* has been translated as a ṣaṣṭhī-tatpuruṣa compound assuming that the prior compound-member *brahman* refers to the creator god Brahmā from whom Vibhīṣaṇa requests it when offered a boon by him. This seems to be the interpretation of the term the text itself implies. However, the term may be a karmadhāraya compound with the prior compound-member referring to sacred text. It would then denote a weapon consisting of a sacred formula. Interpreted analogously, the compound *prajñāstra* would refer to a weapon consisting of consciousness, knowledge, or intelligence. The term 'weapon' for something which consists of a recited sacred formula or knowledge is inappropriate. The term *astra* which it translates, derived from the verbal root √*as* 'throw,' is literally something thrown or impelled. If *astra* is translated 'impulse' in these two compounds, *prajñāstra* would designate a specific mental impulse, and *brahmāstra* a specific textual impulse with the restorative and destructive effects the text describes for them (273.5, 271.16, 274.27–31).

Many of the special abilities referred to are acquired, either by the performance of Vedic ceremonies or by spiritual practice. Indrajit acquires his invincibility by performing a Vedic ceremony to Agni. Thus Vibhīṣaṇa advises Lakṣmaṇa to attack Indrajit before he has completed his morning rites (3.273.16–17). Indrajit mounts his invisible chariot after presenting offerings to Agni in a Vedic ceremony (*R.* 6.67.4–10) because he was granted the special ability (*siddhi*) to be immortal in battle upon doing so by Brahmā in exchange for releasing Indra whom he had vanquished (*R.* 7.30.8–13). Rāma discovers Nala's ability to make whatever he throws in the ocean float when the ocean god propitiated by him in a Vedic ceremony appears to him in a dream and tells him of it (267.32–33).

The Rākṣasa siblings Rāvaṇa, Kumbhakarṇa, and Vibhīṣaṇa acquire their abilities by undertaking spiritual practice for a thousand years while Khara and Śūrpaṇakhā serve and protect them. (259.15–20). Rāvaṇa stood on one foot eating only air, amidst five fires, very collected. The term *susamāhita* used to describe Rāvaṇa's state is related to the term *samādhi* given precise significance in Patañjali's *Yogasūtra* 3.3 as a designation for the most profound state of settled awareness. After a thousand years Rāvaṇa cut off his head and offered it in the fire. Kumbhakarṇa slept only on the ground, restricting his food, observing a vow. Vibhīṣaṇa ate only one withered leaf, fasted, always intent upon muttered recitation. Brahmā, pleased with this, went there himself and caused them to desist from spiritual practice by enticing them all individually with the offering of boons such as lack of bodily deformity, the ability to bear whatever form one wishes, and victory over foes (259.21–31.). Due to his dullness, Kumbhakarṇa chooses long sleep (259.28). Vibhīṣaṇa chooses unwavering virtue and Brahmā's weapon and is offered immortality in addition.

The *Rāmopākhyāna* mentions the spiritual practice of others as well and a few times describes the diet of the practitioners as consisting of fruit and roots (262.1, 31, 264.42). Rāma, Lakṣmaṇa, and Sītā resort to the forest in the garb of spiritual practitioners, except that the former two bear their bows (261.37). They live in a hermitage (258.2, 262.15, 39, 263.15, 22) and visit the hermitage of Śarabhaṅga. They slay Rākṣasas to protect spiritual practitioners in Daṇḍaka's forest (261.42). Due to Rāma's defense of spiritual practitioners in the forest in his youth, Rāvaṇa's former minister Mārīca resorted to the life of a spiritual practitioner in Gokarṇa (3.261.54–55, 3.262.6–7, *R.* 3.37). The monkeys searching the south come upon the female spiritual practitioner Prabhāvatī (266.40). Sītā spots hermitages as she is being abducted (263.7) and continues the life of a spiritual practitioner in Rāvaṇa's captivity (264.41, 266.58).

The text utilizes a few terms which, while meaning 'successful' in any sense, are often used to indicate spiritual attainment. It uses the terms *kṛtakṛtya* and *kṛtārtha* to mean 'successful' in the ordinary sense to describe the monkeys sent south to search for Sītā when they find her and to describe servants who have accomplished their goal (266.28). It uses the term *kṛtakarman* as an epithet of the particularly accomplished and virtuous individuals Vibhīṣaṇa (273.5), Indrajit (273.15), and Aṅgada (275.57). Finally, it uses the term *siddha* to refer to a class of beings mentioned along with sages, gods, and semidivine beings. Siddhas are sometimes described in other texts as semidivine beings inhabiting the atmosphere or some level of heaven. Derivationally, the term means 'accomplished, fulfilled, perfected' and is often used of those endowed with special abilities which are termed *siddhi* (*YS.* 3.37).

3. Transcending and enlightenment

The story of Rāma including its divine dimension directly presents Rāma, as the incarnation of the transcendent, self-existent, omnipotent god Viṣṇu saving the world from the evil demon Rāvaṇa who torments it. It directly presents the transcendent divine responding to the crisis on earth by manifesting itself. It describes Viṣṇu as the supreme self (*puruṣa*) and Sītā, whose name means 'furrow' and whom her father Janaka describes as born from the earth (*R.* 1.65.14–15), as taken captive by Rāvaṇa. It ends with Rāma recognizing his identity with Viṣṇu. The *Uttarakāṇḍa* of the *Rāmāyaṇa* describes Rāma reentering the body of Viṣṇu, and Sītā reentering the earth in her mother's arms. As such the story presents a spiritual metaphor on the individual and collective scales.

On the individual scale, it presents a metaphor for the liberation of the individual self (*ātman*) held captive by ignorance. Rāma represents pure consciousness (*puruṣa*) which is localized transcendental unbounded pure consciousness; Sītā represents the individual body, senses, mind, and intellect which are the manifest evolutes of original nature (*prakṛti*); and Rāvaṇa represents ignorance expressing itself in attachment and desire. The individual self, ignorant of its nature as unbounded pure consciousness, identifies itself with body, senses, mind, and intellect, becomes attached to these localized values, and by its partiality to them is bound in the net of dualities such as desire and aversion, pleasure and pain, etc. In this state, the individual intellect, mind, senses, and body are held captive by the ignorant ego overcome with desire, while the self struggles to liberate them. When ignorance is destroyed, the self recognizes its identity with the transcendent pure consciousness, and the evolutes of nature are freed from the realm of duality and restored to their original pure unmanifest state. This is the state of enlightenment (*kaivalya*) described in *Yogasūtra* 4.34.

On the collective scale, the story of Rāma presents a metaphor for the establishment of a golden age on earth. The *Rāmāyaṇa* directly describes the ten thousand years of Rāma's rule as full of happiness, prosperity, bounty, and long life and as free of suffering, poverty, illness, crime, and violence (*R.* 6.116.80–90). Metaphorically, Sītā represents life on earth bound by suffering and social ills which Rāvaṇa represents. Rāma represents the manifestation of the transcendent pure consciousness in collective awareness. His reign represents the establishment of an age of enlightenment bringing the descent of heaven on earth.

The story of Rāma directly describes the incarnation of Rāma in response to the plea of the gods and sages subjected to the crisis of Rāvaṇa wreaking havoc upon the world. Metaphorically, transcendent pure consciousness becomes manifest to restore balance in response to people turning their attention inwards towards the transcendent. This turning the attention inwards is often inspired by suffering at the time of greatest imbalance.

The scene of Rāma's rejection of Sītā vividly displays the appearance of the gods in response to Sītā's complete surrender in the face of her intense sorrow. It is strikingly reminiscent of the experience of unbounded pure consciousness opening to awareness in the process of transcending.

When Avindhya presents Sītā to Rāma and asks him to accept her back (275.6–7), Rāma descends from his chariot, looks at Sītā in her car beautiful but emaciated by grief, caked with filth, and cloaked in black, and, suspicious of Rāvaṇa's violation of her, rejects her (275.8–10). Rejected, Sītā falls to the earth pallid (275.14–15). The monkeys become motionless and their breaths become still (275.16). In the process of transcending, awareness collecting itself and settling down withdraws from active states of awareness. As it does so, the activity of the body quiets down. As the activity of the body settles, the breathing comes to rest and the mind becomes still. Just at the moment of stillness, the pure-spirited god, Brahmā, the creator of the world reveals himself to Rāma (275.17), accompanied by the whole host of gods, including the lords of the elements, the lord of death, and the lord of wealth. The whole atmosphere becomes bright (275.18–20). When the mind becomes still in the process of transcending, transcendental pure consciousness (*brahman*) reveals itself to the individual awareness and the awareness fills with lustre. When Sītā stands up again (275.21) and asks the elements beginning with Vāyu 'wind' to release her life-breaths if she has sinned (275.23–24), Vāyu's voice resounds in the atmosphere, vouching for her purity and asking Rāma to accept her (275.25–26). The other gods follow suit. Bowing to the gods, Rāma unites with his wife (275.38). As a result of transcending, the body becomes rejuvenated, and activity becomes successful.

The scene of Rāma's rejection of and reunification with Sītā serves as a metaphor of stages in the growth to enlightenment as well as for the process of transcending. In the stage of enlightenment known as cosmic consciousness (*kaivalya*), the self, identified with pure consciousness, recognizing its own purity, views the body and other evolutes of nature as belonging to the field of change from which it dissociates itself. However, in the ultimate stage of development of consciousness (*brahman*), the self recognizes the transcendent original pure state of nature in all the active states of nature and embraces all levels of nature as one with itself.

II

A note on the text and translation

The text translated here is that included in P. M. Scharf (*Rāmopākhyāna: the story of Rāma in the Mahābhārata*) and P. M. Scharf (*Rāmopākhyāna: the story of Rāma in the Mahābhārata*). This text departs from the text of the critical edition of the *Mahābhārata* in several instances. The two three-line verses 276.6–7 have been redistributed into three two-line verses because the last line of verse 6 and the first line of verse 7 form a single sentence. The verses have been renumbered accordingly. In 276.11, the reference to Rāma's companions has been changed to state that Rāma slays Rāvaṇa and recovers Sītā with companions (*sasahāyena*) rather than without companions (*asahāyena*). In several other instances (259.24, 264.41, 267.3, 6, 9, 35, 275.4, 39), a reading in the critical notes has been adopted over the text of the critical edition. Interested readers may refer to the notes on these verses in my edition just mentioned.

The present translation stays as close as possible to the Sanskrit while yet maintaining proper and conventional English prose. It therefore often parallels the Sanskrit quite exactly, for example preserving direct quotation, preserving participles and retaining particles such as 'and, so, for, therefore, indeed'. On the other hand, it occasionally uses secondary discourse to translate direct quotation, often translates clauses containing a sequence of participles by conjoining clauses containing finite verbs, and usually drops the demonstrative pronoun in the main clause coordinated with a relative clause as is the norm in English. Objective complements are translated as the predicates in subordinate clauses. For example, "...knew that he was angry" rather than "...knew him to be angry." A multi-verse sentence is translated by keeping the translation of each verse under its own verse as far as possible. However, where English doesn't permit it, the whole multi-verse sentence is translated under the final verse.

Translation

Mahābhārata
Āraṇyakaparvan
Adhyāya 257
Yudhiṣṭhira's lament over the abduction of Kṛṣṇā

Janamejaya said:
1. After they became severely afflicted because Kṛṣṇā had been abducted in this way, what did the tiger-like sons of Pāṇḍu do next?

Vaiśaṁpāyana said:
2. After he liberated Kṛṣṇā and conquered Jayadratha in this way, Yudhiṣṭhira, the king Dharma, sat with multitudes of seers.
3. In the middle of those great seers listening and commiserating, the delighter of Pāṇḍu (Yudhiṣṭhira) spoke this speech to Mārkaṇḍeya.
4. I consider that time is strong and what is done by the gods is meted out according to rules and what is to be for beings has no deviation.
5. For how could such an occurrence touch our dharma-knowing, dharma-practicing wife, as an undeserved theft, a pure man?
6. For the daughter of Drupada (Kṛṣṇā) did not do any evil or action censured anywhere; always among brahmans, she properly carried out great dharma.
7. The dull-witted king Jayadratha forcefully abducted her. Because of abducting her, he got his head shaved and got defeated in battle with his companions.
8. Thus we took her back after slaying that army of Sindhu. But undisputedly we did get our wife abducted.

9. Miserable is this dwelling in the forest, living on hunting, injury by us forest-dwellers to the forest-dwelling species of animals, and exile by our falsely resolved relatives.
10. Is there now any man less fortunate than I, one you might have seen before or even heard of before?

Mahābhārata
Āraṇyakaparvan
Adhyāya 258
Rāmopākhyāna Adhyāya 1
The birth of Rāma and Rāvaṇa

Mārkaṇḍeya said:
1. O bull among the descendants of Bharata (Yudhiṣṭhira), Rāma attained unparalleled sorrow. His wife, the daughter of Janaka (Sītā), was abducted by the very powerful Rākṣasa. . .
2. . . . Rāvaṇa, the lord of the Rākṣasas from the hermitage through the atmosphere, having resorted to illusion by his power, having slain the vulture Jaṭāyu.
3. Rāma took her back having resorted to the army of Sugrīva, after building a bridge over the ocean and burning Laṅkā with sharp arrows.

Yudhiṣṭhira said:
4. In which family was Rāma born? How courageous was he? How audacious? And whose son was Rāvaṇa? What was his gripe with him?
5. O fortunate one (Mārkaṇḍeya), you can tell me all this completely. I want to hear the conduct of Rāma of impeccable deeds.

Mārkaṇḍeya said:
6. There was a great king Aja by name, born in the line of Ikṣvāku. His son Daśaratha was pure, ever devoted to his daily recitation.

7. He had four sons skilled in right action and polity, Rāma, Lakṣmaṇa, Śatrughna, and the mighty Bharata.
8. Rāma's mother was Kausalyā but Kaikeyī was Bharata's. Lakṣmaṇa and Śatrughna were the two enemy-scorching sons of Sumitrā.
9. Janaka was the king of Videha. Sītā, Rāma's dear queen, whom the Creator himself made, was his daughter, O lord (Yudhiṣṭhira).
10. The birth of Rāma and of Sītā has been related to you; I will describe to you the birth of Rāvaṇa too, O lord of the people (Yudhiṣṭhira).
11. Rāvaṇa's grandfather was actually the god Prajāpati, the self-existent, very radiant, mighty creator of all the worlds.
12. Pulastya, by name, was his beloved, mind-born son. His mighty son, Vaiśravaṇa by name, was born of Go.
13. Abandoning his father, he attended on his grandfather. Because of his anger, O king (Yudhiṣṭhira), his father created himself by himself.
14. Angry, he took birth with half of himself as the twice-born Viśravas to get revenge against Vaiśravaṇa.
15. But his grandfather, pleased with him, granted Vaiśravaṇa immortality, lordship of wealth, and guardianship of a quarter...
16. ...likewise friendship with Īśāna, and a son, Nalakūbara, and Laṅkā endowed with hosts of demons as his capital seat.

Mahābhārata
Āraṇyakaparvan
Adhyāya 259
Rāmopākhyāna Adhyāya 2
The obtainment of boons by Rāvaṇa and his siblings

Mārkaṇḍeya said:

1. The sage Viśravas, who was the half body of Pulastya transformed out of anger, beheld Vaiśravaṇa with anger.
2. But the lord of the demons (Vaiśravaṇa) knew that his father was angry. Kubera was always striving to appease him, O king (Yudhiṣṭhira).
3. The king of kings, having a man as his vehicle, dwelling in Laṅkā, gave three demonesses to be his father's attendants.
4. Then, O tiger among the descendants of Bharata (Yudhiṣṭhira), skilled in dance and song, they undertook to satisfy that great-souled sage, . . .
5. . . . (they) the slender-waisted Puṣpotkaṭā, Rākā, and Mālinī, in mutual competition, desirous of good, O king, lord of the people (Yudhiṣṭhira).
6. Pleased with them, the fortunate great-souled one (Viśravas) bestowed boons, sons like the guardians of the quarters, as desired by each.
7. In Puṣpotkaṭā were born two sons, lords of demons, Kumbhakarṇa and the ten-necked (Rāvaṇa), unparalleled in strength on earth.

8. Mālinī gave birth to one son, Vibhīṣaṇa. In Rākā was born the pair of twins Khara and Śūrpaṇakhā.
9. Now Vibhīṣaṇa excelled them all in appearance. He was fortunate, a protector of dharma, devoted to Vedic performances.
10. But the ten-necked (Rāvaṇa) was the eldest of them all, a bull-like Rākṣasa, of great endurance, virility, character and courage.
11. Kumbhakarṇa excelled them all in strength, a night-ranger possessing special powers, skilled in battle, and violent.
12. Khara was advanced in the bow, a brahman-hating flesh-eater. And Śūrpaṇakhā too was likewise a violent obstructer of Siddhas.
13. All were Veda-knowing heroes, all performed their vows well. They lived devotedly with their father (Viśravas) on Mount Gandhamādana.
14. Then they saw Vaiśravaṇa there, borne by a man, united with supreme wealth, sitting with their father.
15. But, envious, afterwards they became firmly resolved on spiritual practice. Then they pleased Brahmā with their awful spiritual practice.
16. For a thousand years, the ten-necked (Rāvaṇa) stood on one foot eating only air, amidst five fires, very collected.
17. Kumbhakarṇa slept only on the ground, restricting his food, observing a vow. Vibhīṣaṇa ate only one withered leaf.
18. Delighted in fasting, wise, noble-minded, always intent upon muttered recitation, he undertook intense spiritual practice for the same length of time.
19. Khara and Śūrpaṇakhā, cheerful-minded, served and protected them performing spiritual practice.
20. But when a thousand years had passed, the difficult to attack, ten-headed one (Rāvaṇa) cut off his head and offered it in the fire. The lord of the world was pleased with this.
21. After that Brahmā went there himself and caused them to desist from spiritual practice by enticing them all individually with the offering of boons.

Brahmā said:

22. "I am pleased with you. Desist! Choose boons, little children. Let whatever you want except one thing, immortality, be so.

23. Each head of yours which has been offered in the fire with the desire to attain something great–they will be just as they were on your body, as desired.
24. And there will not be any deformity in your body and you will be able to bear any form you wish. And you will be the conqueror of your enemies in battle, there is no doubt."

Rāvaṇa said:
25. "May I not be defeated by Gandharvas, gods, demons, Yakṣas, Rākṣasas, serpents, Kiṁnaras or ghosts."

Brahmā said:
26. "You have fear of none of those whom you have mentioned, but of a man. A blessing to you. Thus it has been ordained by me."

Mārkaṇḍeya said:
27. When he had been addressed thus, the ten-necked one (Rāvaṇa) became satisfied. For the ill-minded man-eater despised humans.
28. Then the great-grandfather (Brahmā) spoke to Kumbhakarṇa in just the same way. He chose long sleep because his consciousness was swallowed by dullness.
29. After saying, "It will be so," he said to Vibhīṣaṇa again and again, "Choose a boon, son; I am pleased."

Vibhīṣaṇa said:
30. "Even if I have come upon the utmost disaster, may I not think of injustice; and, O fortunate one (Brahmā), let Brahmā's weapon, untaught, appear to me."

Brahmā said:
31. "O emaciator of enemies (Vibhīṣaṇa), because your intellect does not rejoice in injustice, even though you have been born in the womb of a demoness, I grant you immortality."

Mārkaṇḍeya said:
32. But after he obtained his boon, O lord of the people (Yudhiṣṭhira), the ten-necked demon (Rāvaṇa) conquered the lord of wealth (Vaiśravaṇa) in battle and drove him from Laṅkā.

33. The blessed (Vaiśravaṇa) left Laṅkā and went to Mount Gandhamādana followed by the Gandharvas and Yakṣas, accompanied by the Rākṣasas and the Kiṁpuruṣas.
34. Rāvaṇa attacked and took his airship Puṣpaka. Vaiśravaṇa cursed him, "This will not carry you.
35. But it will carry only him who will slay you in battle. Because you despise Brahmā and me, soon you will cease to exist."
36. But, O great king (Yudhiṣṭhira), the virtuous Vibhīṣaṇa, endowed with supreme radiance, remembering the dharma of the good, followed (Vaiśravaṇa).
37. Pleased, his wise brother, the fortunate lord of wealth (Vaiśravaṇa), granted his brother (Vibhīṣaṇa) command over the Yakṣa and Rākṣasa armies.
38. The man-eating demons and the mighty fiends all convened and consecrated the ten-headed (Rāvaṇa) king.
39. But the ten-necked (Rāvaṇa), abounding in strength, assuming any form at will, traversing the sky, attacked and took the riches of the Daityas and of the gods.
40. He is called Rāvaṇa because he made the regions cry (√*ru*). The ten-necked (Rāvaṇa), having whatever power he wished, spread terror among the gods.

Mahābhārata
Āraṇyakaparvan
Adhyāya 260
Rāmopākhyāna Adhyāya 3
The birth of the gods in the form of monkeys and bears

Mārkaṇḍeya said:
1. Then the brahman sages, the Siddhas, the gods, and the royal sages placed the oblation-bearer (Agni) before them and went to Brahmā as their refuge.

Agni said:
2. "The mighty ten-headed son of Viśravas (Rāvaṇa), whom your holiness (Brahmā) previously made unslayable by granting him a boon, ...
3. ... that mighty one is harassing all creatures with offenses. Therefore, save us, O fortunate one (Brahmā), for there is no other savior."

Brahmā said:
4. "O shining Vasu (Agni), he is not able to be conquered in battle by gods and demons. Therefore, I have ordained what is necessary to be done for his removal.
5. For that purpose by my command the four-armed Viṣṇu, best of warriors, has descended into human form. He will accomplish this deed."

Mārkaṇḍeya said:

6. Then the grandfather (Brahmā) said this speech in their presence, "Take birth on the surface of the earth together with all the hosts of gods.
7. Progenerate heroic sons possessing whatever forms and powers they desire in all the female bears and monkeys to be Viṣṇu's comrades."
8. Then all the gods, Gandharvas, and Dānavas became eager to descend to the earth quickly with a greater or lesser portion of themselves.
9. In their presence, the boon-granting god (Brahmā) instructed the female Gandharva named Dundubhī so that the object to be accomplished by the gods would succeed.
10. Then after hearing the grandfather's speech, the female Gandharva Dundubhī became the hump-backed Mantharā in the human world.
11. And all the most excellent gods, Indra and so on, progenerated sons in the best female monkeys and bears. They all took after their fathers in glory and strength.
12. Breakers of mountain-peaks, using Śāla trees, Palms, and stones for weapons, all were as solid as the thunderbolt; all likewise as powerful as floods.
13. They all bore whatever virility they wished, were skilled in battle, had the life-breaths of ten thousand elephants, were equal to the speed of the wind in swiftness, and dwelt wherever they wished. Some were forest-dwellers here.
14. When he had thus ordained all that, the fortunate fosterer of the world (Brahmā) informed Mantharā of everything she had to do and how to do it.
15. She acknowledged the order and did accordingly swift as the mind, going hither and thither, intent upon the inflammation of hostilities.

Mahābhārata
Āraṇyakaparvan
Adhyāya 261
Rāmopākhyāna Adhyāya 4
The departure of Rāma, Lakṣmaṇa, and Sitā to the forest

Yudhiṣṭhira said:

1. Your holiness has told the birth of Rāma and the others individually. I want to hear, O brahman (Mārkaṇḍeya), the reason for their departure. Let it be narrated.

2. How were the two heroic sons of Daśaratha, the brothers Rāma and Lakṣmaṇa, banished to the forest, O brahman (Mārkaṇḍeya), and the glorious princess of Mithilā (Sītā)?

Mārkaṇḍeya said:

3. King Daśaratha, delighting in Vedic performances, devoted to dharma, ever mindful of his elders, was pleased when sons were born to him.

4. And gradually those sons of his grew very vigorous, fully conversant in the Vedas together with the Upaniṣads and in the science of archery.

5. When they completed their study and took wives, O king (Yudhiṣṭhira), then Daśaratha was pleased and happy.

6. The eldest of them was Rāma, so called because he delighted the people; intelligent, he satisfied his father's heart with his charm.

7. Then the thoughtful king, considering himself advanced in age, consulted with his counselors and his dharma-knowing Vedic officiants.
8. All those excellent ministers, O descendant of Bharata (Yudhiṣṭhira), considered it high time for the consecration of Rāma as crown prince.
9–13. When he beheld his son, red-eyed, great-armed, going like an elephant in rut, long-armed, broad-chested, dark-curly-haired, shining with radiance, a hero, not inferior to Indra in strength, fully conversant in all dharmas, equal to Bṛhaspati in thought, thoroughly loved by the subjects, proficient in all the sciences, master of his senses, pleasing to the sight even of his enemies, restrainer of the wicked, protector of the virtuous, steadfast, unassailable, an undefeated conqueror, increasing the bliss of Kausalyā, king Daśaratha became supremely pleased, O delighter of the Kurus (Yudhiṣṭhira).
14. Being pleased by reflecting upon the qualities of Rāma, the brilliant heroic one (Daśaratha) addressed his Vedic officiant (Vasiṣṭha), "A blessing to you."
15. O Brahman (Vasiṣṭha), tonight the lunar asterism Puṣya will approach an auspicious conjunction. Let the materials be collected for me, and let Rāma be summoned.
16. When she heard about the king's command, Mantharā went to Kaikeyī and said this speech in time.
17. O Kaikeyī, today the king has declared your great misfortune. O unfortunate lady, an angry, cruel, venomous snake is biting you.
18. Fortunate indeed is Kausalyā, whose son will be consecrated. For whence will good fortune come to you, whose son does not share in the kingdom?
19. When she had understood that speech, she approached her husband in private adorned in all her ornaments, bearing an excellent figure, seeming to have a waist as thin as an altar's, . . .
20. . . . as if laughing, smiling innocently, feigning affection, and spoke the sweet sentence:
21. "O king true to your promises (Daśaratha), deliver the wish which you bestowed upon me. Free yourself from that straight."

The king (Daśaratha) said:
22. "Certainly I shall grant you the boon. You shall receive what you wish. What innocent man shall be executed today? What criminal shall be set free today?
23. To whom shall I grant wealth today or from whom shall it be taken back, whatever possession is mine except the property of brahmans here."

Mārkaṇḍeya said:
24. When she heard that speech, she embraced the lord of men (Daśaratha) and, realizing her power, then said to him:
25. "Let the consecratory ceremony which you planned for Rāma take place for Bharata and let the descendant of Raghu (Rāma) go to the forest."
26. O best of the descendants of Bharata (Yudhiṣṭhira), when he heard that disagreeable, horrifying speech, the king, plunged in sorrow, did not say anything at all.
27. Then, when he ascertained that his father had been so requested, the heroic, virtuous Rāma set out for the forest so that the king would remain true.
28. Then the glorious bow-bearing Lakṣmaṇa followed him as did Rāma's wife Sītā, the princess of Videha, the daughter of Janaka; blessed be she!
29. After that, when Rāma had gone to the forest, king Daśaratha united with the body's transitory nature.
30. But when she ascertained that Rāma had left and likewise that the king had departed, the queen Kaikeyī had Bharata brought back and said to him:
31. "Daśaratha has gone to heaven; Rāma and Lakṣmaṇa are staying in the forest. Seize the vast, comfortable kingdom from which the thorns have been removed."
32. The virtuous one (Bharata) said to her, "Alas, you have committed a cruel deed, by slaying your husband and unseating this family because you were greedy for wealth."
33. He said, "O my mother, family-wrecker, having heaped ignomy on my head, be satisfied!" and wept.

34. Then he cleansed his reputation in the presence of all the subjects and went after his brother Rāma desirous to make him return.
35. Sending Kausalyā, Sumitrā, and Kaikeyī in the vanguard with vehicles, he went, very sorrowful, accompanied by Śatrughna, ...
36. ... with Vasiṣṭha and Vāmadeva and other sages by the thousands, together with the townsfolk and countryfolk, with the desire to bring Rāma back.
37. He saw Rāma accompanied by Lakṣmaṇa in Citrakūṭa wearing the adornment of spiritual practitioners, carrying his bow.
38. Dismissed by Rāma carrying out the word of his father, he administered the kingdom in Nandigrāma placing Rāma's sandals before himself.
39. But Rāma, fearing that the townsfolk and countryfolk would come again, entered the great wilderness at Śarabhaṅga's hermitage.
40. After paying his respects to Śarabhaṅga, he resorted to Daṇḍaka's forest. Then he dwelt beside the lovely Godāvarī river.
41. Then Śūrpaṇakhā caused a great conflict between Rāma dwelling there and Khara living in Janasthāna.
42. And the descendant of Raghu (Rāma), concerned for dharma, slew fourteen thousand Rākṣasas on the earth for the protection of the spiritual practitioners.
43. By slaying the very powerful Dūṣaṇa and Khara himself, the wise descendant of Raghu (Rāma) made it a safe forest of dharma again.
44. But then, when those Rākṣasas had been slain, Śūrpaṇakhā, whose nose and lips had been cut, went to Laṅkā, the home of her brother.
45. Then, blind with sorrow, the demoness (Śūrpaṇakhā) approached Rāvaṇa and fell at her brother's feet with dried blood on her face.
46. Blind with rage seeing her so mutilated, Rāvaṇa leapt up from his throne furious, grinding his teeth.
47. Then, dismissing his ministers, he said to her in solitude, "Who disregarding and despising me has made you so, good woman?"
48. Who approaches a sharp spear and worships it with all his limbs? Who kindles a fire on his head and, relaxed, sleeps easily?
49. Who kicks a horrible venomous snake here? And who stands touching a maned lion on its teeth?
50. Flames of fire emerged from the pores of him speaking in this way as from the crevices of a tree burning in the night.

51. His sister narrated to him all Rāma's valor: the defeat of the Rākṣasas including that of Khara and Dūṣaṇa.
52. Then, the king resolved upon his duty, consoled his sister, instituted order in the city, and rose upward.
53. He passed beyond Mount Trikūṭa and Mount Kāla and saw the deep-watered, great ocean, the abode of sea monsters.
54. Then the ten-headed one (Rāvaṇa) traversed it and approached Gokarṇa, the undisturbed, beloved place of the great-souled spear-bearer (Śiva).
55. There the ten-headed one (Rāvaṇa) approached his former minister Mārīca, who had previously resorted to the life of a spiritual practitioner out of fear of Rāma.

Mahābhārata
Āraṇyakaparvan
Adhyāya 262
Rāmopākhyāna Adhyāya 5
The slaying of Mārīca and abduction of Sītā

Mārkaṇḍeya said:

1. Now Mārīca, for his part, flustered seeing Rāvaṇa come, honored him with respectful offerings and with fruit, roots, and so on.
2. And the tactful Rākṣasa (Mārīca), sitting beside the diplomatic one (Rāvaṇa) sitting reposed, spoke the courteous speech:
3. "You don't have your natural color. Your city is secure, isn't it? Your subjects love you as before, don't they?
4. And also what is to be accomplished by you in coming here, O lord of the Rākṣasas? Consider it accomplished, even if it is very difficult."
5. Rāvaṇa told him everything done by Rāma but Mārīca, having heard, said to Rāvaṇa briefly:
6. "Enough with your attacking Rāma! For I really know his power. For who is able to endure the rush of arrows of that great-souled one.
7. That very bull-like man is the reason for my departure to the forest. What evil-natured person indicated this gate of destruction to you?"
8. Then Rāvaṇa said to him, threatening him angrily, "If you do not do my command, definitely it will be your death anyway."
9. Mārīca thought, "Death caused by a distinguished person is better. If death is inevitably attained, I will carry out his thought."

10. Then Mārīca answered the lord of the Rākṣasas, "What assistance can I render you; even unwilling, I will do it."
11. The ten-necked one (Rāvaṇa) said to him, "Become a jewel-antlered deer whose hide is bright with gems and go entice Sītā!
12. Certainly Sītā, having noticed you, will urge Rāma. When the descendant of Kakutstha (Rāma) has departed, Sītā will be controllable.
13. Having taken her I will abduct her. Then that fool (Rāma) will cease to exist due to separation from his wife. Render me this assistance!"
14. Thus addressed, Mārīca performed the water ceremony for himself and very sadly followed Rāvaṇa going before him.
15. Then those two went to the hermitage of that Rāma of impeccable deeds and accordingly carried out everything previously planned.
16. Rāvaṇa, having become an ascetic with shaven head, water-pot, and three staves, and Mārīca, having become a deer, approached that place.
17. Mārīca, bearing the form of a deer, showed himself to the princess of Videha (Sītā). That precept-motivated woman urged Rāma after it.
18. Rāma, carrying out her wish, quickly took up his bow, instated Lakṣmaṇa for her protection, and went forth with the desire to catch the deer.
19. Holding his bow, wearing his quiver, sword, arm-guard, and finger-guard, Rāma chased the deer as Rudra the deer constellation Mṛgaśīrṣa.
20. He disappeared. Again there was a glimpse of him. The Rākṣasa, prancing, drew him a long way away. Then Rāma recognized him.
21. The brilliant descendant of Raghu knew that he was a night-ranger (Rākṣasa) having the form of a deer, took an unerring arrow and killed him.
22. Then he, struck by Rāma's arrow, imitating Rāma's voice, cried in a painful tone, "Oh, Sītā, Lakṣmaṇa!"
23. Then the princess of Videha (Sītā) heard that pitiable voice of his. She ran forth in the direction from which the sound came. Then Lakṣmaṇa said to her:
24. "Enough with your fear, timid one (Sītā)! Who will overcome Rāma? After a short time you will see Rāma come, O sweetly smiling one."

25. Thus addressed, beginning to cry, verily struck by a woman's nature, she suspected her brother-in-law, who had the epitome of pure conduct.
26. That good woman, devoted to her husband, began to speak abuse to him, "The time which you wish for in your heart does not exist, fool.
27. I would even take a sword and kill myself by myself or jump from a mountain-peak or enter a fire.
28. But no way would I give up my husband Rāma and stay with you, a base man, like a tigress with a jackal."
29. The virtuous Lakṣmaṇa, devoted to Rāma, covered his ears when he heard such a speech and set out by the way the descendant of Raghu (Rāma) had. He picked up Rāma's trail and ran holding his bow.
30. At this interval, the Rākṣasa Rāvaṇa appeared disguised in ascetic's garb, the unrighteous in the form of the righteous, like fire covered by ashes, desirous to abduct that blameless woman.
31. The dharma-knowing daughter of Janaka noticed that he had arrived and offered him food consisting of fruit and roots, and other things.
32. The bull-like Rākṣasa despised all that, resumed his own form, and gently addressed the princess of Videha:
33. "O Sītā, I am the king of the Rākṣasas famed as Rāvaṇa in name. My pleasant city, Laṅkā by name, is on the other side of the ocean.
34. There you will shine among excellent women with me. Be my wife, O broad-hipped lady! Abandon the spiritual practitioner, the descendant of Raghu!"
35. When she heard these and similar sentences, Sītā, the broad-hipped daughter of Janaka, covered her ears and said, "Do not speak this way!
36. If the sky with the constellations were to fall, if the earth were to break into pieces, if fire were to become cold, I would not abandon the delighter of Raghu (Rāma).
37. For after staying with a split-templed, forest-ranging, spotted great elephant, how could an elephant cow touch a pig?
38. For, I think, after drinking Mādhīka and Madhumādhavī, how could any woman have the desire for sour gruel?"
39. After addressing him thus, she started to enter the hermitage again. Rāvaṇa ran after that broad-hipped woman and prevented her.

40. After threatening her unconscious with a harsh voice, he grabbed her by the hair and then rose into the sky.
41. Then the mountain-ranging vulture Jaṭāyu saw that female spiritual practitioner being abducted, crying, "Rāma, Rāma!"

Mahābhārata
Āraṇyakaparvan
Adhyāya 263
Rāmopākhyāna Adhyāya 6
The slaying of Kabandha

Mārkaṇḍeya said:

1. The mighty Jaṭāyu, whose brother was Saṁpāti, the son of Aruṇa, king of the vultures, was a friend of Daśaratha's.
2. He saw his daughter-in-law Sītā at Rāvaṇa's side then. Out of anger the bird rushed toward Rāvaṇa, the king of the Rākṣasas.
3. Then the vulture said to him, "Release her! Release the princess of Mithilā! How will you take her while I live, night-ranger? For I will not release you alive if you do not let my daughter-in-law go."
4. After speaking thus to the lord of Rākṣasas, he rent him severely with his talons. And he (Rāvaṇa), sorely mutilated by blows of his wings and beak, shed blood plentifully, as a mountain sheds water through its streams.
5. Being struck by the vulture desiring the welfare of Rāma's darling, he took his sword and cut off the wings of that bird.
6. Having struck down the king of the vultures like a mountain with tattered clouds, the Rākṣasa rose upward holding Sītā by his side.
7. But wherever the princess of Videha saw a circle of hermitages, a lake, or a river, she dropped an ornament.
8. She saw five bull-like monkeys on a mountain table-land. There the clever lady dropped a large beautiful garment.
9. Tossed by the wind, that bright yellow cloth fell amidst the five lords of monkeys like lightning amidst the clouds.

10. When the princess of Videha had been abducted in this way, then the wise Rāma, having turned back after slaying the great deer, saw his brother Lakṣmaṇa.
11. Seeing his brother, he rebuked him thus, "Why have you come leaving the princess of Videha in the forest crawling with Rākṣasas?"
12. Then he sickened, considering that he had been drawn away by a Rākṣasa bearing the form of a deer and that his brother had come.
13. But Rāma quickly accosted him rebuking him, "Does the princess of Videha live? I don't see her, Lakṣmaṇa."
14. Lakṣmaṇa told him the entire speech of Sītā, the final improper words which the princess of Videha had spoken.
15. But Rāma flew towards the hermitage with his heart burning. Then he saw the mountain-like vulture struck down.
16. But suspecting a Rākṣasa, the descendant of Kakutstha (Rāma) drew his mighty bow, then ran towards him with Lakṣmaṇa.
17. The brilliant one (Jaṭāyu) said to those two Rāma and Lakṣmaṇa together, "I am the king of the vultures, friend of Daśaratha's. A blessing to you."
18. And they, hearing that speech of his, contracted their glorious bows and said, "Who is this who calls our father by name?"
19. Then they saw him that way, having both of his wings cut. But the vulture told them that he had been smitten by Rāvaṇa for the sake of Sītā.
20. The descendant of Raghu asked the vulture, "Which direction did Rāvaṇa go?" The vulture told him with movements of his head and died.
21. The descendant of Kakutstha (Rāma) having understood that gesture of his to mean towards the south, performed the cremation ceremony honoring the friend of his father.
22. Seeing the site of the hermitage in which the seats and pots had been cast about, in which jars had been smashed, empty, overrun by jackals and crows, . . .
23. . . . the two scorchers of enemies, filled with sorrow and grief, agitated by Sītā's abduction, went south through Daṇḍaka's forest.
24. But in that great forest Rāma, with the son of Sumitrā (Lakṣmaṇa), saw herds of deer running in all directions and heard the awful cry of creatures as if there were a forest fire raging.

25. And after a short time they saw the horrible-looking Kabandha, like a mountain of clouds, broad-shouldered, mighty-armed, with large eyes in his chest and a large mouth in his great belly.
26. Then suddenly that Rākṣasa grabbed Lakṣmaṇa in his hand. At once, O descendant of Bharata (Yudhiṣṭhira), the son of Sumitrā (Lakṣmaṇa) became despondent.
27. He looked at Rāma as he was drawn towards his mouth and said despairingly to Rāma, "Look at this situation of mine!"
28. The princess of Videha was abducted, I am perishing, you fell from the kingdom, and our father died.
29. I will not see you reunited with the princess of Videha, returned to Kosala, reestablished in your ancestral kingdom on earth.
30. Fortunate are they who will see the face of the prince consecrated with grass, parched grain, and Śamī-logs, like the moon with tatters of clouds.
31. Variously in this way did the wise Lakṣmaṇa wail. Then the descendant of Kakutstha (Rāma), unperturbed in the midst of turmoils, said to him:
32. "Don't grieve, O tiger-like man! This is nobody as long as I am present. Cut off his right arm! I have cut off his left."
33. Speaking thus, Rāma felled his (Kabandha's) arm, cut with his very sharp sword, like a sesame stalk.
34. Then the mighty son of Sumitrā (Lakṣmaṇa), seeing his brother the son of Raghu (Rāma) present, smote his (Kabandha's) right arm with his sword.
35. Lakṣmaṇa smote that Rākṣasa again forcefully on the side. Then, the enormous Kabandha fell to the ground lifeless.
36. A person of divine appearance emerged from his body, resorted to the sky and was seen blazing like the sun in the sky.
37. Rāma asked him courteously, "Who are you? Speak to one asking with desire. What is this strange thing? It appears wonderful to me?"
38. To him he said, "I am the Gandharva Viśvāvasu, O king (Rāma). I attained a womb served by a Rākṣasa due to the curse of a brahman.
39. Sītā was abducted by Rāvaṇa, the king dwelling in Laṅkā. Go to Sugrīva; he will give you assistance.
40. This is the auspicious-watered Pampā, resorted to by geese and ducks, winding within its banks near Mount Ṛśyamūka.

41. Sugrīva, brother of the golden-garlanded monkey-king Vālin, lives here with four associates.
42. This much we can tell you: you will see the daughter of Janaka. The monkey-king certainly knows Rāvaṇa's abode."
43. Having said this, the very radiant divine person disappeared and both the heroes Rāma and Lakṣmaṇa were astonished.

Mahābhārata
Āraṇyakaparvan
Adhyāya 264
Rāmopākhyāna Adhyāya 7
The consolation of Sītā by Trijaṭā

Mārkaṇḍeya said:

1. Then Rāma, plunged in sorrow over the abduction of Sītā, reached the river Pampā nearby, filled with blue and red lotuses.

2. Being succored by a pleasant cool breeze bearing the fragrance of ambrosia in that forest, he went with his mind to his darling.

3. Remembering his beloved there, pained by the arrow of love, that lord of kings (Rāma) lamented. Then the son of Sumitrā (Lakṣmaṇa) said to him:

4. "This sort of emotion is not able to touch you, O bestower of confidence, as disease is not able to touch a man of healthy habits, possessed of the self.

5. You have received news of the princess of Videha and of Rāvaṇa. Rescue her by human effort and intelligence!

6. Let's go to the bull-like monkey Sugrīva on the mountain. Have confidence in me your disciple, servant, and companion."

7. When he had been addressed in this way by Lakṣmaṇa with expressions of many kinds, the descendant of Raghu (Rāma) regained his constitution and became focused on what had to be done.

8. After worshipping the water of the Pampā and pouring water as an offering to their deceased ancestors too, the two heroes, the brothers Rāma and Lakṣmaṇa, set out.
9. When they came to R̥śyamūka, the mountain abounding in roots and fruit, the two heroes saw five monkeys on the mountain-top.
10. Sugrīva sent them his monkey associate, the wise Hanūmat, stable like the Himālayan range.
11. After conversing with him first, they went to Sugrīva. Then, O king (Yudhiṣṭhira), Rāma established friendship with the monkey-king.
12. When he had made known his purpose, they showed him the garment which Sītā had dropped to the monkeys while being abducted.
13. When he found the monkey-lord Sugrīva providing that assurance, Rāma himself spoke of consecrating him to lordship of the monkeys on earth.
14. The descendant of Kakutstha (Rāma) committed to the slaying of Vālin in battle and Sugrīva, to the recovery of the princess of Videha, O king (Yudhiṣṭhira).
15. When they had spoken thus, contracted an agreement, and encouraged each other, they all went to Kiṣkindhā and stood desirous of battle.
16. When he reached Kiṣkindhā, Sugrīva roared with a sound like a flood. Vālin did not tolerate it from him. Tārā checked him:
17. "The way Sugrīva roars, this monkey is powerful, and I think he has come with support. You should not go out."
18. Then her husband, the eloquent lord of the monkeys, the golden-garlanded Vālin, said to Tārā whose face was like the lord of the stars:
19. "Look you, knowing the speech of all beings, endowed with intelligence! With whom as support has this pseudo-brother of mine arrived?"
20. But after thinking for a moment, the intelligent Tārā, radiant as the lord of the stars, said to her husband, "Hear everything, O lord of the monkeys!
21. The great-souled bowman Rāma, Daśaratha's son, whose wife had been abducted, formed an alliance with Sugrīva.
22. And his brother, the great-armed, undefeated, intelligent son of Sumitrā, Lakṣmaṇa by name, stands ready to accomplish the goal.

23. And Sugrīva's ministers Mainda, Dvivida, Hanūmat, son of the wind, and Jāmbavat, king of the bears, are present.
24. Great-souled, intelligent, and mighty, they are all able to destroy you by resorting to Rāma's power."
25. Rejecting that speech of hers which had been spoken for his benefit, the lord of monkeys jealously suspected her of being concerned about Sugrīva.
26. After speaking harshly to Tārā, he emerged from the mouth of the cave. To Sugrīva who was standing near Mount Mālyavat, he said:
27. "Fool, more than once I released you who are dear to me as life even though I had beaten you because I considered that you were my relative. What is your hurry for death again?"
28. Thus addressed, the enemy-slaying Sugrīva told his brother this portentous speech, as if alerting Rāma that the time had arrived.
29. "O king (Vālin), know that I have come considering that I am hardly fit to live since you have taken my wife and kingdom."
30. After saying many sorts of things in this way then Vālin and Sugrīva fell in together in combat using Śāla trees, Palm trees, and stones as weapons.
31. Both struck each other; both fell down on the ground. Both leapt wonderfully and struck each other with their fists.
32. Then, wounded by claws and teeth, sprinkled with blood, both heroes shone like blossomed Kiṁśuka trees.
33. No difference between them was seen then in the battle. Then Hanūmat put a garland on Sugrīva's neck.
34. Then that hero shone with the garland attached to his neck like the bright, great mountain range, the Malaya, with its garland of clouds.
35. But when he saw that Sugrīva had been marked, the great-bowed Rāma drew his most excellent bow, aiming at Vālin as target.
36. The bow trembled like a catapult. Then Vālin trembled, struck by the arrow in his heart.
37. Struck in a broken vital spot, vomiting blood from his mouth, he saw Rāma standing at a distance with the son of Sumitrā (Lakṣmaṇa).
38. He censured the descendant of Kakutstha (Rāma) and fell on the ground unconscious. Tārā saw him fallen on the ground like the lord of the stars.

39. When Vālin had been slain, Sugrīva returned to Kiṣkindhā and to her whose lord had fallen, Tārā, whose face was like the lord of the stars.
40. But the wise Rāma dwelt for four months on the bright top of Mount Mālyavat, attended by Sugrīva.
41. Now Rāvaṇa went to his city Laṅkā and, agitated by the strength of his desire, settled Sītā within his Nandana-like palace, near an Aśoka grove which was like a spiritual practitioner's hermitage.
42. There that wide-eyed girl spent sorrowful nights, thin-limbed because of remembering her husband, wearing the dress of a female spiritual practitioner, accustomed to fasting and spiritual practice, observing a diet of fruit and roots.
43. To guard her there, the lord of the Rākṣasas assigned the female Rākṣasas, bearing darts, swords, spikes, axes, hammers, and firebrands, . . .
44. . . . Two-eye, Three-eye, Forehead-eye, Long-tongue, Tongueless, Three-breast, One-foot, Triple-braid (Trijaṭā), and One-eye.
45. These and other flaming-eyed female Rākṣasas, having hair is as thick as the trunk of an elephant, were sitting surrounding Sītā ceaselessly day and night.
46. Those violent dreadful-sounding demonesses, pronouncing their consonants and vowels harshly, were continually threatening that long-eyed girl:
47. "Let's eat her! Let's tear this woman who lives here despising our master apart, dividing her bit by bit!"
48. To them threatening her thus, being frightened again and again, filled with grief on account of her husband, sighing, she said this:
49. "O noble ladies, eat me quickly! I have no desire to live without that lotus-eyed, dark-curly-haired man (Rāma).
50. Besides, without food, separated from him who is dear as life, I will dry out my limbs like a cat in a Palm tree.
51. But know the truth about me: I would not approach another man besides the descendant of Raghu (Rāma). Be done what follows!"
52. After hearing that speech of hers, those harsh-voiced female Rākṣasas went to tell it all to the lord of the Rākṣasas from the beginning.
53. When they had all gone, the dharma-knowing, sweet-speaking female Rākṣasa named Trijaṭā consoled the princess of Videha:

54. "Sītā, I will tell you something; have confidence in me, friend. Let your fear depart, fair-thighed one, and listen to this speech of mine:
55. There is an intelligent, aged, bull-like Rākṣasa named Avindhya. He is Rāma's well-wisher. For he told me for your sake:
56. 'Sītā should be told by my word, after consoling and soothing her, "Your strong husband Rāma, followed by Lakṣmaṇa, fares well.
57. The glorious descendant of Raghu (Rāma) has made an alliance with the monkey-king, brilliant as Indra, and is endeavoring for your sake.
58. And don't be afraid of Rāvaṇa reviled by the world, O timid lady. For you, blameless one, are protected by Nalakūbara's curse.
59. Because this evil slave to the senses (Rāvaṇa) was cursed when he assaulted (his nephew Nalakūbara's) bride Rambhā, he cannot approach an unwilling woman.
60. Your wise husband will come quickly protected by Sugrīva, accompanied by the son of Sumitrā (Lakṣmaṇa) and will liberate you from here.
61. For I have seen very awful ugly dreams portending the destruction of this evil-minded destroyer (Rāvaṇa) of the family of the son of Pulastya (Vaiśravaṇa).
62. For this ill-natured, mean, night-ranger is dreadful, increasing fear in all out of his own nature because of a character-fault.
63. I have seen signs of the destruction of that one who, having his consciousness afflicted by time, vies with all the gods.
64. Many times the ten-headed (Rāvaṇa) is standing as if dancing on a chariot yoked with donkeys, anointed with sesame oil, bald, sinking in mud.
65. And these Kumbhakarṇa and so on are being drawn in the southern direction, naked, bald, and garlanded and anointed in red.
66. Vibhīṣaṇa alone turbaned, with white garland and ornaments, under a white parasol, atop a white mountain...
67. ...and his four ministers garlanded and anointed in white atop a white mountain are being spared from this great horror.
68. The earth with its oceans is surrounded by Rāma's missile. Your husband will fill the whole earth with glory.
69. And I saw Lakṣmaṇa atop a heap of bones eating rice-pudding, surveying all directions.

70. Many times I saw you crying, with your limbs drenched in blood, going in the northern direction, protected by a tiger.
71. O Sītā, princess of Videha, pretty soon you will be happy, quickly united with your husband, the descendant of Raghu, along with his brother."""
72. After hearing that speech of Trijaṭā, that fawn-eyed girl (Sītā) became hopeful for reunion with her husband.
73. When the violent, very dreadful demonesses arrived, they saw her sitting with Trijaṭā as before.

Mahābhārata
Āraṇyakaparvan
Adhyāya 265
Rāmopākhyāna Adhyāya 8
The dialogue between Sītā and Rāvaṇa

Mārkaṇḍeya said:
1–2. Then Rāvaṇa, afflicted by the arrow of love, saw her abiding with the female Rākṣasas, sitting on a stone slab, afflicted with grief on account of her husband, distressed, wearing a soiled garment, having her bridal necklace as her only ornament, crying, devoted to her husband, and he approached her.
3. Unconquered in war by gods, Dānavas, Gandharvas, Yakṣas, and Kiṁnaras, he went to the Aśoka grove, confounded by love.
4. Wearing beautiful clothes, radiant, wearing earrings of polished jewels, having colorful garlands and crown, he was like spring embodied.
5. Even arduously decorated like the wish-granting tree, he was terrifying even adorned, like a tree growing on a funeral mound in a cemetery.
6. That night-ranger next to that thin-waisted one looked like the planet Saturn approaching the constellation Rohiṇī.
7. After greeting that beautiful-hipped lady, struck by the arrow of love, he said this to the girl powerless like a trembling red doe:
8. "O Sītā, this is enough. You have done your obligation to your husband. Be gracious, slim-limbed one. Let your toilette be done!
9. Love me, O beautiful-hipped lady, wearing precious ornaments and dresses. Be the highest of all my wives, noble lady!

10. I have maidens of the gods and women of the royal-sages. I have maidens of the Dānavas and girls of the Daityas.
11. A hundred and forty million demons stand at my command; twice as many man-eating Rākṣasas of frightful deeds.
12. I have three times as many Yakṣas who carry out my commands; only a few have resorted to my brother the overseer of wealth (Vaiśravaṇa).
13. Gandharvas and Apsarases, good lady, always wait on me in my dining hall, just as on my brother in his, O fair-thighed one.
14. I am also directly the son of the brahman-seer and sage Viśravas. The rumor has spread about me that I am the fifth of the guardians of the quarters.
15. O radiant lady, I have divine foods and victuals and various drinks just like those of the lord of the thirty (Indra).
16. Let the unpleasant effect caused by your dwelling in the forest be destroyed. Be my wife, beautiful-hipped lady, like Mandodarī."
17. Thus addressed by him, the beautiful-faced princess of Videha, covered herself, put a blade of grass between them and said to that night-ranger.
18. The young princess of Videha, of exceedingly lovely thighs, devoted to her husband, incessantly drenching her two firm, contiguous breasts with inauspicious tears told that vile one this speech:
19. "Unfortunately I have heard this sort of despondent speech from you, O lord of the Rākṣasas, more than once.
20. O blessed and happy one, a blessing to you. Let that desire of yours be checked. I am another's wife, unobtainable, and ever devoted to my husband.
21. Moreover, a pitiable human wife would not be suitable for you. And what pleasure will you obtain by assaulting an unwilling woman?
22. Your father was a sage, born of Brahmā, equal to a Prajāpati. Why don't you protect dharma like a guardian of a quarter?
23. But how are you not ashamed of this, taking the place of your powerful brother, the lord of wealth, king of kings, friend of the great lord?"
24. Having said this, covering her face with her garment, the slender-limbed Sītā began to cry, undulating her breasts and neck.

25. The long, well-arranged braid of that radiant one crying appeared like a very dark, glossy black snake on her head.
26. After hearing that very harsh speech spoken by Sītā, the foolish Rāvaṇa continued his speech, even though rejected:
27. "Let the Makara-bannered god of love burn my limbs as much as he wants, Sītā; I will not unite with you whose hips are beautiful and smile is charming, if you are unwilling.
28. What can I do if even today you stick just to Rāma, the human, our food."
29. After saying this to that irreproachable-limbed one, the lord of the host of Rākṣasas disappeared on the spot and went in the direction he wanted.
30. Then surrounded by female Rākṣasas, emaciated by grief, being attended upon by Trijaṭā, the princess of Videha, dwelt right there.

Mahābhārata
Āraṇyakaparvan
Adhyāya 266
Rāmopākhyāna Adhyāya 9
The return of Hanūmat

Mārkaṇḍeya said:

1. But the descendant of Raghu (Rāma), accompanied by the son of Sumitrā (Lakṣmaṇa), protected by Sugrīva, dwelling on top of Mount Mālyavat, beheld the clear sky.

2. That slayer of enemies (Rāma), having seen the pure moon followed by the planets, constellations, and stars in the clear sky, . . .

3. . . . standing on the mountain, was suddenly alerted by the cool breeze bringing the fragrance of white water lilies, blue lotus blossoms, and day lotuses.

4. In the morning the virtuous one (Rāma), dispirited, said to the hero Lakṣmaṇa after remembering Sītā captive in the Rākṣasa's dwelling:

5. "Go Lakṣmaṇa! Know that the lord of the monkeys in Kiṣkindhā is distracted by domestic duties, ungrateful, and clever in his own aims, . . .

6. . . . that low-born fool whom I caused to be consecrated in kingship, whom all the cowtail monkeys and bears serve, . . .

7. . . . for whose sake I slew Vālin then in the grove near Kiṣkindhā with you, O mighty-armed upholder of the family of Raghu.

8. I consider him ungrateful, an outcast of monkeys on earth, who thus situated now deluded does not know me, O Lakṣmaṇa.

9. I think he does not understand the fulfillment of an agreement, surely because he despises me since I have provided him assistance.

10. If indeed he lies inactive, lustful and hedonistic, you should lead him by the path of Vālin to the destination of all beings.
11. But if the bull-like monkey is intent upon our purpose, take him and come, descendant of Kakutstha (Lakṣmaṇa)! Be quick! Don't delay!"
12. Thus addressed by his brother, intent upon carrying out the word of his elder, Lakṣmaṇa took his splendid bow with arrows and bowstring and set out. He reached the door to Kiṣkindhā and entered unobstructed.
13. Thinking that he was angry, the well-bred monkey, king Sugrīva, lord of monkeys, went up to him with his wife. He received him pleasantly with honor befitting him.
14. Fearless, the son of Sumitrā (Lakṣmaṇa) told him Rāma's speech. Having heard it all completely, bowing, folding his hands in reverence, . . .
15. . . . , O lord of kings (Yudhiṣṭhira), the lord of monkeys, Sugrīva, accompanied by his wife and servants, pleasantly said this speech to the excellent man, Lakṣmaṇa:
16. "I am not foolish, Lakṣmaṇa, nor ungrateful, nor cold. Hear the effort which I have undertaken in search of Sītā.
17. I have dispatched all the well-trained monkeys to the directions. The time has been set to return in a month for all of them. . .
18. . . . by whom, O hero, this earth with its forests, mountains, villages, cities and mines, surrounded by the oceans, is to be searched.
19. That month should be completed in five nights. Then you will hear something very dear along with Rāma."
20. Thus addressed by the wise lord of monkeys, Lakṣmaṇa, relieved, abandoned his wrath and honored Sugrīva in return.
21. Accompanied by Sugrīva, he went to Rāma staying on the top of Mount Mālyavat and reported back to him the result of his job.
22. Thus the lords of monkeys who had searched three directions came together by the thousands, but not those who had gone south.
23. They related to Rāma that they had searched the earth, girdled by the ocean, but had not seen the princess of Videha or Rāvaṇa.
24. But hopeful about the bull-like monkeys who had gone in the southern direction, the descendant of Kakutstha (Rāma) sustained his life-breaths even though afflicted.

25. When two months' time had passed, then monkeys approached Sugrīva and hurriedly said:
26. "The great lush honey-grove Madhuvana which has been protected by Vālin and by you, O best of monkeys, is being eaten by the son of the wind (Hanūmat), . . .
27. . . . and by Vālin's son Aṅgada and the other bull-like monkeys which you dispatched, O king (Sugrīva), to search the southern direction."
28. Hearing that behavior of theirs, he (Sugrīva) considered that they were successful. For this is the conduct of servants who have achieved their aim.
29. That intelligent bull-like monkey (Sugrīva) told it to Rāma. And Rāma too inferred that Sītā had been seen.
30. The monkeys headed by Hanūmat, refreshed, approached the lord of monkeys (Sugrīva) in the presence of Rāma and Lakṣmaṇa.
31. Seeing Hanūmat's gait and complexion, Rāma became more certain that Sītā had been discovered, O descendant of Bharata (Yudhiṣṭhira).
32. But the monkeys headed by Hanūmat, fulfilled, bowed properly to Rāma, Sugrīva, and Lakṣmaṇa.
33. Rāma took up his bow and arrows and said to them when they had arrived, "Will you inspire me to live? Have you been successful?
34. Will I govern the kingdom in Ayodhyā again after slaying my enemies in battle and recovering Janaka's daughter?
35. Without having liberated the princess of Videha and slain my enemies in battle, I cannot bear to live disgraced by having had my wife abducted."
36. To Rāma having spoken thus the son of the wind (Hanūmat) replied, "I shall tell you something dear, Rāma: I have seen the daughter of Janaka.
37. Tired after searching the southern direction with its mountains, forests, and mines, just when the time had passed, we saw a large cavern.
38. But we entered it, extending many yojanas, dark, very unsteady, deep, infested with insects.
39. After going a very long way towards the light of the sun, then we saw right there, inside, a divine castle.

40. It was the abode of the Daitya, Maya himself, O descendant of Raghu. There a female spiritual practitioner named Prabhāvatī was performing spiritual practice.
41–42. Restored after eating the edibles and various drinks she gave us, we went out according to her direction by the path she indicated and saw beside the saline sea the Sahya and Malaya mountain ranges and the great Mount Dardura.
43. Having climbed the Malaya, looking at Varuṇa's abode (the ocean), downcast, agitated, afflicted, completely hopeless about life, ...
44. ... very sorrowful considering the ocean extending for many hundreds of yojanas, the abode of whales, crocodiles and fish, ...
45. ... then we were sitting there having resolved not to eat. Then, at the end of a story, there was the story of the vulture Jaṭāyu.
46. Then we saw a terrifying bird of awful form like a mountain-peak, like another son of Vinatā (Garuḍa).
47. He intended to eat us, then after approaching said, 'Sir, Who is this who is telling the story of my brother Jaṭāyu?
48. I am his eldest brother Saṁpāti by name, the lord of the birds. In competition with each other, we climbed to the assembly of the sun.
49. Then these two wings of mine were burnt but Jaṭāyu's were not burnt. Since then it has been a long time since I have seen my dear brother, the lord of vultures; for I fell with incinerated wings on this great mountain.'
50. We informed him speaking thus that his brother had been slain and briefly informed him of this your lordship's misfortune.
51. Then, O king, enemy-tamer (Rāma), after hearing the very disagreeable news, despondent, Saṁpāti questioned us again.
52. 'Who is Rāma? How was Sītā abducted? And how was Jaṭāyu slain? I want to hear all this, most excellent monkeys.'
53. I told him all this, your lordship's arrival of misfortune and the reason for our sitting in a fast unto death, in detail.
54. That king of birds made us stand up with this sentence, 'Rāvaṇa is known to me and Laṅkā, his great city, ...
55. ... has been seen by me on the other side of the ocean, in a valley on Mount Trikūṭa. Sītā is there; I have no doubt about this.'
56. Having heard his speech, we stood up quickly and consulted about a plan for leaping over the ocean, O scorcher of enemies (Rāma).

57. When no one resolved to leap across the ocean, then I (Hanūmat) entered my father (the wind) and floated across the ocean extending for hundreds of Yojanas, slaying a water-demoness.
58. There I saw Sītā in Rāvaṇa's women's apartments, dedicated to fasting and spiritual practice, longing for the sight of her husband, having matted locks and limbs smeared with dirt, thin, distressed, a spiritual practitioner.
59. After ascertaining that it was Sītā by means of various signs, having approached, I went up to her in an isolated spot and said to the noble lady:
60. 'Sītā, I am Rāma's messenger, a monkey, the son of the wind. Desirous to obtain the sight of you, I have come here through the air.
61. The two brothers, the princes Rāma and Lakṣmaṇa, fare well protected by Sugrīva, the lord of all the monkeys.
62. Rāma, with the son of Sumitrā (Lakṣmaṇa), sends greeting and, because of being his friend, Sugrīva asks you about your welfare.
63. Your husband will come quickly with all the monkeys. Trust me, queen, I am a monkey not a Rākṣasa.'
64. And after thinking for a moment, Sītā answered me, 'I know from Avindhya's speech that you are Hanūmat.
65. For, O mighty-armed, Avindhya is a Rākṣasa respected by elders. He told me about Sugrīva surrounded by ministers like you.'
66. And telling me, 'Go!' Sītā presented this jewel by which the blameless princess of Videha has been sustained through this time.
67. And for the sake of proof, because it serves as a cause of recognition, O tiger-like man, Janaka's daughter narrated this story, that your lordship cast an arrow at the crow on the great mountain Citrakūṭa.
68. Then after causing myself to be heard and then burning that city, I came back." Rāma honored him telling this dear news.

Mahābhārata
Āraṇyakaparvan
Adhyāya 267
Rāmopākhyāna Adhyāya 10
The building of the bridge to Laṅkā

Mārkaṇḍeya said:

1. Then while Rāma was sitting there with them, the best of the monkeys gathered at Sugrīva's command.
2. The glorious father-in-law of Vālin, Suṣeṇa, surrounded by ten billion swift monkeys, approached Rāma.
3. And the two mighty monkey-lords Gaja and Gavaya were seen each surrounded by a billion.
4. O great king (Yudhiṣṭhira), the frightful-looking, cow-tailed Gaākṣa was seen leading six hundred billion.
5. But the Gandhamādana-dweller famed as Gandhamādana led ten billion ferocious monkeys.
6. The very strong, intelligent monkey named Panasa led five hundred and seventy million.
7. The glorious and heroic monkey-elder named Dadhimukha led a great army of frightfully brilliant monkeys.
8. Jāmbavat was seen with a trillion streak-faced black bears of frightful deeds.
9. O great king (Yudhiṣṭhira), these and many other innumerable monkey-generals gathered on Rāma's account.

10. The tumultuous sound of them looking like Śirīṣa flowers running hither and thither was heard like that of roaring lions.
11. Some looking like mountain-peaks, some like buffalo, like autumn clouds, or having their faces smeared with vermilion-paste, . . .
12. . . . other monkeys jumping up, falling down and bounding, gathered from everywhere, raising the dust.
13. Then that great world of monkeys, looking like the full ocean, made camp there at the behest of Sugrīva.
14. When those monkey-lords had gathered from everywhere, on a date in an auspicious nakṣatra, at a celebrated hour, . . .
15. . . . Then the glorious descendant of Raghu (Rāma) went forth accompanied by Sugrīva seeming to shake the worlds with that arrayed army.
16. But Hanūmat, the son of the wind, was the vanguard of the army. The fearless son of Sumitrā (Lakṣmaṇa) protected the rear.
17. The two descendants of Raghu (Rāma and Lakṣmaṇa) wearing wrist and finger guards shone surrounded by the excellent monkeys like the sun and moon surrounded by the planets.
18. That monkey-army, armed with Śāla trees, Palm trees, and stones, appeared like a very extensive rice-field at sunrise.
19. That very great army protected by Nala, Nīla, Aṅgada, Krātha, Mainda, and Dvivida went to accomplish the goal of the descendant of Raghu (Rāma).
20–21. Properly camping without trouble in commended lands abounding in roots and fruit, abounding in honey and meat, containing water, and propitious, and likewise on mountain-ridges, then the monkey-army approached the saltwater ocean.
22. Then like a second ocean, that many-bannered army secured the coastal forest and set up camp.
23. Then Daśaratha's glorious son (Rāma) addressed to Sugrīva in the midst of the monkey-principals this timely speech:
24. "What means have you considered for crossing the ocean? This is a large army and the ocean is difficult to cross."
25. Some monkeys considering themselves wise said, "But monkeys are not able to leap over the entire sea."
26. Some resolved to cross by means of ships, some by various rafts. But Rāma gently answered them all, "No.

27. Not all the monkey heroes are able to jump across the ocean extending for hundreds of Yojanas. This determination of yours is not definitive.
28. Likewise, the army does not have many ships to convey it across. And how could someone like us deal a blow to the merchants?
29. And surely the enemy would strike our widely spread out army in its weak points. And crossing by means of rafts and boats does not please me here.
30. But I will win over this ocean by technique. I will implore him fasting; then he will show me a way.
31. If he will not show me a way, then I will burn him with unimpeded great missiles exceeding the blaze of fire and wind."
32. Having spoken thus, then the descendant of Raghu accompanied by the son of Sumitrā (Lakṣmaṇa) touched water and implored the ocean properly on a bed of Kuśa grass.
33. But then the ocean god, the glorious lord of rivers and streams, surrounded by hosts of sea monsters, showed himself to the descendant of Raghu (Rāma) in a dream.
34. Covered by mines of gems by the hundreds, he addressed him (Rāma), "O son of Kausalyā," and spoke this sweet speech:
35. "Tell me, O bull-like man! What service shall I do for you here. For I am a descendant of Ikṣvāku, your relative." Rāma said to him:
36. "O lord of rivers and streams, I want a way for the army to be given, having gone by which I may slay the ten-necked one (Rāvaṇa), destroyer of Pulastya's son (Vaiśravaṇa).
37. If your lordship will not present a way to me asking thus, I will dry you up with arrows consecrated with divine missiles."
38. When he heard Rāma speaking thus, the abode of Varuṇa (the ocean), agitated, standing with folded hands, said:
39. "I do not desire your obstruction; I am not your obstructor. And hear this speech, Rāma. After hearing it do what you must.
40. If I give you a way for your marching army at your command, others will command me in this way by force of their bow too.
41. But there is here a strong monkey respected by artisans, Nala by name, the son of the fashioner god, Viśvakarman.
42. I will support everything that he throws in me, wood, grass or stone. That will be your bridge."

43. When he had disappeared after saying this, Rāma said to Nala, "Build a bridge over the ocean; for I think you are able to."
44. By that means the descendant of Kakutstha (Rāma) had a bridge constructed ten Yojanas wide, a hundred Yojanas long...
45. ...which even today, widely known on earth as Nala's bridge, mountain-like, is sustained out of respect for Rāma's command.
46. The virtuous Vibhīṣaṇa, the brother of the lord of Rākṣasas (Rāvaṇa), with four ministers, approached him (Rāma) present there.
47. The great-minded Rāma received him with welcome even though Sugrīva had the suspicion that he might be a spy.
48. When the descendant of Raghu (Rāma) was completely satisfied about his true nature by his behavior, deeds and gestures, then he honored him.
49. Moreover, he consecrated Vibhīṣaṇa in kingship over all Rākṣasas and made him his counselor and Lakṣmaṇa's friend.
50. And upon the advice of Vibhīṣaṇa, he traversed the ocean with the army by that bridge in just a month, O overlord of men (Yudhiṣṭhira).
51. Then he went, reached and had the monkeys destroy the great and many gardens of Laṅkā.
52. Two Rākṣasas, Rāvaṇa's ministers Śuka and Sāraṇa, were there in the form of monkeys as spies. Vibhīṣaṇa captured them.
53. When those two night-rangers had resumed their Rākṣasic form, then Rāma showed them to the army and later released them.
54. After encamping the army in a grove, then the hero (Rāma) dispatched the wise monkey Aṅgada as an envoy to Rāvaṇa.

Mahābhārata
Āraṇyakaparvan
Adhyāya 268
Rāmopākhyāna Adhyāya 11
The first assault on Laṅkā

Mārkaṇḍeya said:

1. The descendant of Kakutstha (Rāma) encamped the army in that forest abounding in food and water, filled with roots and fruit, and protected it properly.

2. And Rāvaṇa established order in Laṅkā as prescribed by the treatises. It was difficult to attack by nature, having strong ramparts and portals.

3. There were seven deep-water moats filled with fish and crocodiles, difficult to attack, built with piles made from Khadira wood.

4. They were difficult to attack because of catapults, had iron bars and rocks, were guarded by soldiers with pots of venomous snakes, and were coated with resin, potion, and dust...

5. ...and were endowed with clubs, firebrands, iron arrows, spears, swords and axes, and with hundred-slayers, and with beeswax-coated mallets.

6. There were stationary and moving defenses abundant in infantry, plentiful in elephants and horses at all the city-gates.

7. But then Aṅgada having arrived at the gateway of Laṅkā, having been acknowledged by the Lord of Rākṣasas (Rāvaṇa), entered fearlessly.

8. Amidst many ten-millions of Rākṣasas, the very mighty one (Aṅgada) shone like the sun surrounded by garlands of clouds.

9. He (Aṅgada) approached the son of Pulastya (Rāvaṇa) surrounded by his ministers, saluted him and began to speak Rāma's message eloquently.
10. O king (Rāvaṇa), the glorious descendant of Raghu, lord of Kosala, tells you this timely speech. Accept it and do it!
11. Countries and cities perish when they become filled with imprudence after obtaining an unevolved king devoted to imprudence.
12. You alone have transgressed against me by forcefully taking Sītā. That will result in the slaying of others who have not transgressed.
13. Filled with strength and arrogance, you have previously injured seers wandering in the forest and also have insulted the gods, ...
14. ... slain royal sages and abducted women weeping. Now the result of that imprudence of yours has caught up with you.
15. I will slay you together with your ministers. Fight! Be a man! O Rākṣasa, behold the power of the bow of me, a human.
16. Let Sītā the daughter of Janaka be freed! If you will not free her for me at all, I will make this world devoid of Rākṣasas with my sharp arrows.
17. Infuriated hearing the caustic speech of that envoy speaking thus, king Rāvaṇa did not tolerate it.
18. Then understanding the gestures of their lord, four night-rangers grabbed him on his four limbs like birds, a tiger.
19. Taking those night-rangers holding onto his limbs, Aṅgada leapt up in the air and alighted on the roof of the palace.
20. While he was rising quickly, those night-rangers fell to the ground broken-hearted, hurt by the impact.
21. Freed, he leapt down again from the palace-roof, bounding over the city of Laṅkā, to the vicinity of his own army.
22. Then after approaching the lord of Kosala (Rāma) and reporting everything, the glorious Aṅgada rested, applauded by the descendant of Raghu (Rāma).
23. Then the delighter of Raghu (Rāma) had Laṅkā's rampart breached by a total assault of the wind-swift monkeys.
24. Then Lakṣmaṇa, placing Vibhīṣaṇa and the king of the bears (Jāmbavat) in front, broke down the unassailable southern city-gate.
25. Then he fell upon Laṅkā with a trillion monkeys, whose limbs were tan and like the trunks of elephants, distinguished in battle.

26. Then the sun was not seen, its light obscured by the dust caused by the monkeys jumping up, jumping around, and jumping down.
27–28. But the Rākṣasas with their women and elders, astonished, saw the rampart completely turned orange everywhere with rice-blossom-like, Śirīṣa-flower-like reed-white monkeys having the color of the young sun, O king (Yudhiṣṭhira).
29. They broke the jeweled-pillars and catapult-tops and cast apart the machines whose efficacy had been broken and destroyed.
30. And grasping the hundred-slayers with their wheels, iron bars, and rocks, the mighty ones threw them with the swiftness of their arms into the middle of Laṅkā.
31. Then the few troops of night-rangers who were standing on the rampart fled by the hundreds attacked by the monkeys.
32. But then, by the king's command, the Rākṣasas, who can adopt an appearance at will, came out changed in form by the multitudes of hundred thousands.
33. Raining showers of weapons, driving away the forest-dwellers, clearing the ramparts, they resorted to supreme valor.
34. The rampart was made free of monkeys again by the frightful-looking, bean-pile-colored night-rangers.
35. Many bull-like monkeys fell, their bodies cloven by spears, and night-rangers fell there, crushed by pillars and portals.
36. The battle of the Rākṣasas with the monkeys was carried on by grabbing each other on the hair and by claws and teeth of the heroes biting each other.
37. Monkeys and Rākṣasas, both crying out, slain, fallen to the ground, did not release each other there.
38. But Rāma rained lattices of arrows like a cloud. Reaching Laṅkā, they slew the night-rangers.
39. The firm-bowed son of Sumitrā (Lakṣmaṇa) too, victorious over fatigue, continuously aimed at and felled Rākṣasas in the citadels with his arrows.
40. Then there was a withdrawal of the armies by command of the descendant of Raghu (Rāma). He was predominantly victorious, having gained his goal, a blow having been delivered against Laṅkā.

Mahābhārata
Āraṇyakaparvan
Adhyāya 269
Rāmopākhyāna Adhyāya 12
The battle between the pairs Rāma and Rāvaṇa, etc.

Mārkaṇḍeya said:

1. Then several troops of Piśācas and cruel Rākṣasas, followers of Rāvaṇa, attacked those soldiers resting,
2. Parvaṇa, Pūtana, Jambha, Khara, Krodhavaśa, Hari, Praruja, Aruja, Praghasa, and the like.
3. Then Vibhīṣaṇa, recognizing them, struck down the invisibility of those invisible evil-natured ones attacking.
4. They, being seen by the strong, long-leaping monkeys, altogether slain, O king (Yudhiṣṭhira), fell to the earth lifeless.
5. Not tolerating it, then Rāvaṇa marched out with his army. Having mustered it in the formation of Uśanas, he attacked all the monkeys.
6. But the descendant of Raghu (Rāma), having marched out towards the ten-necked one (Rāvaṇa), drew up in battle array against the night-ranger making the formation of Bṛhaspati.
7. Then having encountered him, Rāvaṇa fought with Rāma there and Lakṣmaṇa likewise with Indrajit, . . .
8. . . . Sugrīva with Virūpākṣa and Nikharvaṭa with Tāra, Nala with Tuṇḍa there and Paṭuśa with Panasa.

9. Each having engaged whomever he considered vincible, fought with him at the time of battle, having resorted to the strength of his own arms.
10. That battle grew awful, hair-raising, terrifying the timid, as formerly did the battle between the gods and the demons.
11. Rāvaṇa reached Rāma with showers of spears, spikes, and swords, and Rāma, Rāvaṇa with sharp, whetted iron arrows.
12. Likewise Lakṣmaṇa pierced the persevering Indrajit with arrows splitting his vital spots, and Indrajit pierced the son of Sumitrā with many arrows.
13. Fearless, Vibhīṣaṇa showered Prahasta, and Prahasta, Vibhīṣaṇa, with sharp, bird's feather arrows.
14. There was a collision of those strong, great weapons because of which all three moving and unmoving worlds trembled.

Mahābhārata
Āraṇyakaparvan
Adhyāya 270
Rāmopākhyāna Adhyāya 13
The emergence of Kumbhakarṇa

Mārkaṇḍeya said:

1. Then Prahasta, harsh in battle, suddenly came up to Vibhīṣaṇa, roared and struck him with his mace.

2. The wise, great-armed one (Vibhīṣaṇa), struck by that frightfully swift mace, did not budge, stable as the Himālaya.

3. Then Vibhīṣaṇa took up a large hundred-bell, consecrated that great missile and threw it at his head.

4. The Rākṣasa was seen decapitated by that thunderous, swiftly falling missile like a tree broken by the wind.

5. Seeing the night-ranger Prahasta slain in battle, Dhūmrākṣa rushed towards the monkeys with great speed.

6. His frightful-looking, cloud-like army fell upon them. Just seeing it, the bull-like monkeys were suddenly scattered in battle.

7. Then seeing those bull-like monkeys suddenly scattered, the tiger-like monkey Hanūmat went out and stood firm.

8. Seeing the son of the wind (Hanūmat) standing in battle, the monkeys regrouped with great speed from all sides, O king (Yudhiṣṭhira).

9. Then a great, tumultuous, hair-raising din arose from the armies of Rāma and Rāvaṇa rushing towards each other.

10. When that awful, bloody and filthy battle began, Dhūmrākṣa put the army of monkeys to flight with his arrows.
11. The rival-conquering Hanūmat, son of the wind, quickly received that excellent Rākṣasa attacking.
12. An awful battle ensued between those two monkey and Rākṣasa heroes wanting to beat each other in fight like Indra and Prahlāda.
13. The Rākṣasa was striking the monkey with maces and bludgeons and the monkey was striking the Rākṣasa with trees together with their boughs and limbs.
14. Then the wise Hanūmat, son of the wind, with his enormous body, slew Dhūmrākṣa together with his horses, chariot, and charioteer.
15. Then, encouraged when they saw the excellent Rākṣasa Dhūmrākṣa struck down, the monkeys attacked and slew his soldiers.
16. Being slain by the strong monkeys shining with victory, the Rākṣasas, disillusioned, fled to Laṅkā out of fear.
17. The surviving night-rangers, having fled to the city broken, informed king Rāvaṇa of everything as it had happened.
18. But when he heard from them that Prahasta and the great archer Dhūmrākṣa along with his army had been slain in battle by the bull-like monkeys, . . .
19. . . . he sighed deeply and jumping up from his throne said, "The time for action has come for Kumbhakarṇa."
20. After saying so, he awoke the slumbering, torpid Kumbhakarṇa with various very loud sounding musical instruments.
21. Having awakened him with great effort, then the alarmed ten-necked lord of the Rākṣasas said to the mighty Kumbhakarṇa siting composed, undisturbed and alert:
22. "Fortunate are you who have this sleep of this kind, who do not know this dreadful, very fearful time.
23. This Rāma, having crossed the sea by means of a bridge with the monkeys, despising us all here, is making a great slaughter.
24. For I abducted his wife, Sītā by name, the daughter of Janaka. Desirous to free her, he has come having constructed a bridge over the ocean.
25. And he has slain our own great kinsmen, Prahasta and others. There is no one else to slay him except you, emaciator of enemies.

26. You yourself march out clad in armor today, best of the strong, and slay all the enemies beginning with Rāma today in battle, O enemy-tamer!
27. And Dūṣaṇa's younger brothers Vajravega and Pramāthin will follow you with a great army."
28. Having spoken thus to the mighty Kumbhakarṇa, the lord of Rākṣasas assigned Vajravega and Pramāthin their duties.
29. The two heroes, Dūṣaṇa's younger brothers, told Rāvaṇa, "Yes," placed Kumbhakarṇa in front and quickly marched out of the city.

Mahābhārata
Āraṇyakaparvan
Adhyāya 271
Rāmopākhyāna Adhyāya 14
The slaying of Kumbhakarṇa, Vajravega and Pramāthin

Mārkaṇḍeya said:

1. Then, having marched out of the city, Kumbhakarṇa with his followers saw the army of monkeys standing before him shining with victory.
2. The monkeys came up to him quickly, surrounded him completely and hit him with many large-trunked trees, and others scratched him with their claws ignoring the perilous danger.
3. Attacking with diverse strategies, the monkeys beat the terrifying lord of Rākṣasas with various weapons.
4. Laughing while being beaten, he ate the monkeys, Panasa, Gaākṣa, and the monkey Vajrabāhu.
5. Tāra and the others cried out trembling when they saw that disturbing deed of the Rākṣasa Kumbhakarṇa.
6. Sugrīva, fearless of Kumbhakarṇa, rushed to Tāra who was crying out loudly, and to the other monkey-troop-leaders.
7. Then the great-minded excellent monkey swiftly leapt towards Kumbhakarṇa and, having struck him on the head forcefully with a Śāla tree, . . .

8. ...the great-souled, swift monkey Sugrīva broke the Śāla on Kumbhakarṇa's head and did not even agitate him.
9. Then having roared, laughing, aroused by the touch of the Śāla tree, Kumbhakarṇa snatched Sugrīva in his arms and took him by force.
10. But the heroic son of Sumitrā (Lakṣmaṇa), the delighter of his friends, saw Sugrīva being taken by the Rākṣasa Kumbhakarṇa and ran up.
11. Having rushed up, Lakṣmaṇa, slayer of enemy heroes, shot a swift, gold-shafted, great arrow at Kumbhakarṇa.
12. The missile pierced his armor and body and spattered with blood went on rending the ground.
13. So, pierced in the heart, the great archer Kumbhakarṇa released the lord of the monkeys and, having taken a boulder as weapon, rushed towards the son of Sumitrā, raising the great boulder.
14. He (Lakṣmaṇa) severed the two upraised arms of that one quickly rushing towards him, with two sharp-tipped razors. He (Kumbhakarṇa) became four-armed.
15. All those arms of his having taken boulders as weapons too, the son of Sumitrā severed with razors, displaying his nimble weapon.
16. He (Kumbhakarṇa) became enormous with many feet, heads, and arms. The son of Sumitrā burned him looking like a heap of boulders with Brahmā's weapon.
17. The mighty one, struck by the divine weapon, incinerated by the great bolt, fell in battle like a tree with branches.
18. Seeing the powerful Kumbhakarṇa Vṛtra-like fallen to the ground lifeless, the Rākṣasas fled from fear.
19. Seeing the warriors running thus, then Dūṣaṇa's younger brothers stopped the son of Sumitrā and rushed towards him angrily.
20. The son of Sumitrā roared and received both Vajravega and Pramāthin, angrily rushing towards him, with arrows.
21. Then, O son of Pṛthā (Yudhiṣṭhira), a very tumultuous, hair-raising battle occurred between Dūṣaṇa's younger brothers and the wise Lakṣmaṇa.
22. He showered the two Rākṣasas with a deluge of arrows and those two angry heroes both showered him.
23. For a period in this way the very severe encounter between Vajravega and Pramāthin and the great-armed son of Sumitrā continued.

24. Then Hanūmat, son of the wind, having picked up a mountain-peak, rushed up and took the life-breaths of the Rākṣasa Vajravega.
25. Then the very strong monkey Nīla ran up and mashed Dūṣaṇa's younger brother Pramāthin with a large boulder.
26. Then occurred again a bitter battle between the armies of Rāma and Rāvaṇa attacking each other.
27. The forest animals slew the sons of Nirṛti (Rākṣasas) and the sons of Nirṛti the forest animals by the hundreds. Mostly the sons of Nirṛti were being slain there but not the monkeys.

Mahābhārata
Āraṇyakaparvan
Adhyāya 272
Rāmopākhyāna Adhyāya 15
Indrajit's felling of Rāma and Lakṣmaṇa

Mārkaṇḍeya said:

1. Then, hearing that Kumbhakarṇa had been slain in battle together with his followers, as well as the great archer Prahasta and the fierce Dhūmrākṣa, . . .

2. . . . Rāvaṇa told his heroic son Indrajit, "Kill Rāma, enemy slayer, and Sugrīva along with Lakṣmaṇa!"

3. For you, my good son, have acquired illustrious fame having conquered the thunderbolt-wielding, thousand-eyed, lord of might (Indra) in battle.

4. Slay the enemies, O enemy-slayer, best of my weapon-bearers, having disappeared or visible, using divine arrows granted as boons!

5. O sinless one, Rāma, Lakṣmaṇa and Sugrīva are not able to bear the touch of your arrows. How can their followers?

6. The revenge for Khara, O sinless one, which was not obtained by Prahasta and Kumbhakarṇa in battle, get it, great-armed one!

7. By slaying my enemies with their soldiers today with whetted shafts, gladden me, son, as you did by binding the chief of the Vasus (Indra).

8. Thus addressed, Indrajit said, "Yes," mounted his chariot clad in armor and went forth quickly to battle, O king (Yudhiṣṭhira).

9. Announcing his name loudly, the bull-like Rākṣasa challenged the lucky Lakṣmaṇa in battle.
10. And Lakṣmaṇa took up his bow and arrows and ran towards him causing trembling by the thump of his soles like a lion chasing small deer.
11. Then a very great intense battle ensued between those two greedy for victory, knowing divine weapons, contending with each other.
12. But when the son of Rāvaṇa (Indrajit) did not pierce him with his missiles, then that best of the strong resorted to greater effort.
13. Then he tormented him with swift javelins. The son of Sumitrā (Lakṣmaṇa) split them as they came with whetted arrows. Cut down with sharp arrows, they fell to the surface of the earth.
14. The radiant Aṅgada, son of Vālin, lifted up a tree, rushed towards him swiftly and struck him on the head.
15. Unperturbed, the mighty Indrajit wanted to strike him in his chest with a spear, but Lakṣmaṇa split that spear of his.
16. When the bull-like monkey, the hero Aṅgada came near, Rāvaṇa's son struck him on the left side with his mace.
17. Disregarding that blow, the strong son of Vālin (Aṅgada), conqueror of enemies, threw the Śāla-tree-trunk angrily at Indrajit.
18. O son of Pṛthā (Yudhiṣṭhira), the tree thrown with fury by Aṅgada to kill Indrajit crushed Indrajit's chariot together with its horses and charioteer.
19. Then, O king (Yudhiṣṭhira), his charioteer killed, Rāvaṇa's son leapt from his chariot whose horses had been killed and disappeared on the spot by his special power.
20. Having realized that the Rākṣasa had disappeared and had many special powers, Rāma came to the place and protected the army.
21. Then he (Indrajit) aimed at and pierced Rāma and the great warrior Lakṣmaṇa in all their limbs with arrows granted as boons.
22. Then the two heroes Rāma and Lakṣmaṇa both fought with arrows Rāvaṇa's invisible son (Indrajit) who had disappeared by his special power.
23. He furiously shot arrows in all the limbs of those two lion-like men again by the hundreds, then by the thousands.
24. Searching for that invisible one shooting arrows incessantly, the monkeys grabbed large stones and entered the sky.

25. The Rākṣasa hero, Rāvaṇa's son (Indrajit), invisible, hidden by his special power, pierced both them and those two with arrows beating them severely.
26. Those two heroes, the two brothers Rāma and Lakṣmaṇa, covered with arrows, fell from the sky to the ground like the sun and moon.

Mahābhārata
Āraṇyakaparvan
Adhyāya 273
Rāmopākhyāna Adhyāya 16
Lakṣmaṇa's slaying of Indrajit

Mārkaṇḍeya said:

1. Seeing both those two brothers of unmeasured vigor fallen, Rāvaṇa's son (Indrajit) bound them more with arrows granted as boons.
2. Those two heroes, tiger-like men, bound by Indrajit with a lattice of arrows in battle appeared like two vultures in a net.
3. Seeing those two fallen on the ground covered with hundreds of arrows, Sugrīva, king of the monkeys, stood surrounding them together with the monkeys, . . .
4. . . . Suṣeṇa, Mainda, Dvivida, Kumuda, Aṅgada, Hanūmat, Nīla, Tāra, and Nala.
5. Then the accomplished Vibhīṣaṇa came to that place and awakened those two heroes made conscious with the missile of consciousness.
6. And Sugrīva made them both free from arrows in an instant with the great medicinal herb Viśalyā employed with sacred formulas.
7. Those two best of men having regained consciousness, free from arrows, stood up and in a moment both great warriors were free from exhaustion and weariness.
8. O son of Pṛthā (Yudhiṣṭhira), when Vibhīṣaṇa saw Rāma, the delighter of Ikṣvāku, free from grief, he said, folding his hands in reverence:

9. "O enemy-tamer, this Guhyaka took water and came to your presence from the White Mountain under the instruction of the king of kings (Vaiśravaṇa).
10. The great king Kubera presents this water to you for the purpose of seeing creatures who have disappeared, O scorcher of enemies.
11. If you touch your eyes with this, you will be able to see creatures who have disappeared, and so will whoever you present it to."
12. Then Rāma accepted that honored water saying, "Yes," and washed his eyes and so did the great-minded Lakṣmaṇa.
13. And so did Sugrīva and Jāmbavat, Hanūmat, Aṅgada, Mainda, Dvivida and Nīla and the majority of the most excellent monkeys.
14. Then what Vibhīṣaṇa said came to be: Their eyes were in a moment clairvoyant, Yudhiṣṭhira.
15. But the accomplished Indrajit, having informed his father of that deed of his, came again with haste to the battle-front.
16. Standing on the advice of Vibhīṣaṇa, the son of Sumitrā ran towards him who was angrily attacking with the desire to fight again.
17. Then Lakṣmaṇa, angry, desirous to slay him who was shining with victory before he had completed his daily rites, having been so advised, struck him with arrows.
18. Then a very extraordinary, wonderful battle ensued between those two desiring to beat each other, like the one between Śakra and Prahlāda.
19. Indrajit pierced the son of Sumitrā (Lakṣmaṇa) with sharp arrows splitting his vital spots and the son of Sumitrā pierced Rāvaṇa's son (Indrajit) with arrows whose touch was like fire.
20. Infuriated by the touch of the arrows of the son of Sumitrā, Rāvaṇa's son (Indrajit) shot eight arrows like venomous snakes at Lakṣmaṇa.
21. Listen to me tell how the heroic son of Sumitrā (Lakṣmaṇa) drew out his (Indrajit's) life breaths with three arrows whose touch was like fire.
22. With one he made his bow-bearing arm fall from his body. With the second he made his arrow-bearing arm fall to the ground.
23. But with the third lustrous broad-edged shaft he took his dear head having a beautiful nose and wearing sparkling earrings.

24. After slaying that frightful-looking cask having the arms severed from the shoulders, the best of the strong (Lakṣmaṇa) slew his charioteer with arrows too.
25. Then his horses drew his chariot into Laṅkā and Rāvaṇa saw that chariot deprived of his son.
26. Seeing his son slain, Rāvaṇa, whose eyes were agitated from fear, fallen into grief and bewilderment, prepared to kill the princess of Videha (Sītā).
27. Taking his sword, the ill-natured one rushed towards her sitting in the Aśoka grove eagerly longing for the sight of Rāma.
28. Listen to the reasoning with which Avindhya calmed the angry one when he saw the evil intention of that fool.
29. "Being in a glorious great kingdom, you cannot kill a woman. And especially when this woman has been killed already and is in bondage in your house.
30. And my opinion is that she would not be killed by the destruction of her body. Slay her husband; she would be slain if he were slain.
31. For not even the god of a hundred rites (Indra) himself is equal to your valor; for you have trounced the thirty gods with Indra in war more than once."
32. Thus with various arguments Avindhya calmed the angry Rāvaṇa, and he accepted his speech.
33. Having made the decision to march out, the night-ranger put away his sword and then commanded, "Let my chariot be prepared."

Mahābhārata
Āraṇyakaparvan
Adhyāya 274
Rāmopākhyāna Adhyāya 17
Rāma's slaying of Rāvaṇa

Mārkaṇḍeya said:

1. Then the ten-headed one (Rāvaṇa), angry since his dear son had been slain, mounted his chariot adorned with gold and gems, and marched out.

2. Surrounded by awful Rākṣasas holding various weapons in their hands, he rushed towards Rāma, overpowering the monkey-troop-leaders.

3. Mainda, Nīla, Nala and Aṅgada, Hanūmat and Jāmbavat, together with their armies surrounded him as he rushed towards them angrily.

4. Those troop-leaders of the bears and monkeys were scattering the army of the ten-necked one (Rāvaṇa) with trees while he was watching.

5. Then seeing his own army being slain by the enemies, Rāvaṇa, the lord of the Rākṣasas, possessing special powers, effected his special power.

6. Then Rākṣasas were seen after emerging from his body by the hundreds and by the thousands holding arrows, spears, and swords in their hands.

7. Rāma, slew all those Rākṣasas with a divine missile. Then the lord of the Rākṣasas effected his special power even more.

8. O descendant of Bharata (Yudhiṣṭhira), making forms of Rāma and of Lakṣmaṇa, the ten-necked one (Rāvaṇa) rushed towards Rāma and Lakṣmaṇa.

9. Then, O king (Yudhiṣṭhira), as those night-rangers reached Rāma and Lakṣmaṇa, they fell upon them, holding forth their bows raised.
10. Seeing that special power of the lord of the Rākṣasas, Sumitrā's son (Lakṣmaṇa), the delighter of Ikṣvāku, said this great speech to Rāma, unperturbed:
11. "Slay these evil Rākṣasas which are resemblances of yourself!" And Rāma slew those of them which were resemblances of himself.
12. Then Mātali, Indra's charioteer, drew up to Rāma in the battle with a chariot as brilliant as the sun, yoked with bay horses.

Mātali said:
13. "This victorious chariot yoked with bay horses is the ultimate vehicle of the munificent one (Indra). O descendant of Kakutstha (Rāma), tiger-like man, with this best of chariots Indra slew the Daityas and the Dānavas by the hundreds in battle.
14. So with this vehicle guided by me, tiger-like man, quickly slay Rāvaṇa in battle. Don't delay!"
15. Thus addressed, the descendant of Raghu (Rāma) suspected of Mātali's true speech, "This is an illusion of the Rākṣasa (Rāvaṇa)." Vibhīṣaṇa told him:
16. "This is not an illusion of the evil-natured Rāvaṇa, O tiger-like man. So, O very glorious one, mount this chariot of Indra quickly."
17. Then, delighted, the descendant of Kakutstha (Rāma), having said, "Yes," to Vibhīṣaṇa, rushed quickly at the ten-necked one (Rāvaṇa) with the chariot, filled with fury.
18. When Rāvaṇa was attacked, creatures made the sound, "hāhā," and divine lion's roars with kettle drums thundered in the sky.
19. The night-ranger threw a very awful spear like Indra's thunderbolt, like the upraised staff of Brahmā.
20. Rāma split that spear midway with whetted arrows. Seeing that infeasible feat, fear entered Rāvaṇa.
21. Angered, then the ten-necked one quickly discharged whetted arrows and various kinds of swords at Rāma by the ten millions.
22. Then Bhuśuṇḍis, spears, maces, axes, various kinds of lances, and hundred-slayers with sharpened blades.
23. Seeing that strange power of the ten-necked Rākṣasa, all the monkeys fled in all directions from fear.

24. Then the descendant of Kakutstha (Rāma) selected the fine-feathered, fine-headed, gold-shafted, ultimate arrow from his quiver and yoked it with Brahmā's weapon.
25. The gods and Gandharvas headed by Indra rejoiced seeing the best of arrows consecrated with Brahmā's weapon by Rāma.
26. Then because of the discharging of Brahmā's weapon, the gods, Gandharvas, and Kiṁnaras considered the life of the enemy Rākṣasa to be almost over.
27. Rāma released that awesome arrow of unparalleled power like the upraised staff of Brahmā, making an end of Rāvaṇa.
28. By it the best of Rākṣasas, together with his chariot, horses, and charioteer, engulfed by fire, caught fire with a great blaze.
29. Then the thirty gods, together with the Gandharvas and the celestial singers rejoiced seeing Rāvaṇa struck down by Rāma of impeccable deeds.
30. The five elements abandoned the great Rāvaṇa; for he was felled in all worlds by the brilliance of Brahmā's weapon.
31. For his bodily elements, flesh and blood, perished, incinerated by Brahmā's weapon, and not even his ashes were seen.

Mahābhārata
Āraṇyakaparvan
Adhyāya 275
Rāmopākhyāna Adhyāya 18
Rāma's reunion with Sītā, return to Ayodhyā and consecration

Mārkaṇḍeya said:

1. Having slain the cruel, god-hating Rāvaṇa, lord of Rākṣasas, Rāma was delighted, along with Sumitrā's son (Lakṣmaṇa) together with their friends.

2. When Rāvaṇa had been slain, then the gods with the seers as their leaders honored that great-armed one (Rāma) with their congratulations for his victory.

3. All the deities and Gandharvas whose abode is heaven lauded lotus-petal-eyed Rāma with showers of flowers and with praises.

4. After honoring Rāma thus, they returned as they came. The sky looked festival-like, O imperishable one (Yudhiṣṭhira).

5. Then having slain the ten-necked one (Rāvaṇa), the very glorious lord Rāma, conqueror of the enemy-city, presented Laṅkā to Vibhīṣaṇa.

6. Then the very wise aged minister Avindhya came out having placed before him Sītā attended by Vibhīṣaṇa.

7. And he said to the great-souled descendant of Kakutstha (Rāma) sunk in depression, "Accept back your virtuous queen, the daughter of Janaka, O great-souled one."
8. When he heard this speech, the delighter of Ikṣvāku (Rāma) descended from that ultimate chariot and looked at Sītā covered with tears.
9. Seeing her whose every limb was beautiful standing in her vehicle emaciated by grief, having every limb caked with filth, wearing matted locks, and having her garment black, . . .
10. . . . Rāma, suspicious of Rāvaṇa's violation of her, said to the princess of Videha (Sītā), "Go, princess of Videha! You have been freed. I have done what I had to do."
11. I slew that night-ranger so that you, good lady, having obtained me as your husband, would not attain old age in the Rākṣasa's house.
12. For how could someone like me, knowing resolution in dharma, support even for a moment a woman who has been in another man's arms.
13. Chaste or not, I cannot enjoy you now, princess of Mithilā (Sītā), any more than an oblation licked by a dog.
14. When the young princess heard that dreadful speech, she suddenly fell down trembling like a banana tree cut down.
15. The color on her face born from joy vanished again in an instant as if it had arisen from exhalation on a mirror.
16. Then all the monkeys together with Lakṣmaṇa, hearing that spoken by Rāma, became motionless, nearly bereft of their life-breaths.
17. Then the four-faced, pure-spirited god, the grandfather, the creator of the world, revealed himself to the descendant of Raghu (Rāma) with his vehicle, . . .
18. . . . and so did Indra, Agni, Vāyu, Yama, Varuṇa, the fortunate lord of the Yakṣas (Kubera), and the pure seven seers, . . .
19. . . . and king Daśaratha, possessing a divine and radiant form, with his exceedingly worthy, lustrous vehicle yoked with geese.
20. Then the entire atmosphere filled with gods and Gandharvas shone like the surface of the sky bright with stars in autumn.
21. Then the noble princess of Videha stood up glorious in their midst and spoke this speech to the broad-chested Rāma:

22. "Prince, I am not angry at you, for I know the way of women and of men, but listen to my speech.
23. The ever-moving wind god moves within beings. Let him liberate my life-breaths if I have sinned.
24. Let fire, water, space, earth, and wind liberate my life-breaths if I have sinned."
25. Then there was an auspicious voice in the atmosphere resounding in all directions, delighting the great-souled monkeys.

Vāyu said:
26. "O sir, sir, descendant of Raghu, truly I am the ever-moving wind. The princess of Mithilā (Sītā) is sinless, king. Unite with your wife."

Agni said:
27. "I am present within the body of beings, O delighter of Raghu (Rāma). The princess of Mithilā has not gone astray even very minutely, O descendant of Kakutstha (Rāma)."

Varuṇa said:
28. "Verily, the bodily fluids are produced by me in the bodies of beings, O descendant of Raghu (Rāma). Verily, I tell you, 'Take back the princess of Mithilā (Sītā).'"

Brahmā said:
29. "Good son, this is not strange for you, having the dharma of a royal sage and standing on the path of the virtuous, in this situation. But listen to this speech of mine:
30. You, O hero, have felled this enemy of the gods, Gandharvas, and serpents, Yakṣas, Dānavas, and great sages.
31. Previously, by my grace, he became unslayable by all beings. For some reason the evil one was disregarded for some time.
32. That evil-natured one abducted Sītā in order to be slain. And I protected her by means of Nalakūbara's curse.
33. For he was told before that if he should make love to any other unwilling woman, definitely his body would burst into a hundred pieces.
34. You should not be suspicious in this situation. Take her back, O very glorious one. You have carried out a great obligation for the gods, O immortal-like one."

Daśaratha said:
35. "I am pleased, son. A blessing to you. I am your father Daśaratha. I consent. And govern the kingdom, best of men!"

Rāma said:
36. "I greet you, Indra of kings, if you are my progenitor. I will go to the enjoyable city, Ayodhyā, at your command."

Mārkaṇḍeya said:
37. O lord of men (Yudhiṣṭhira), his father told him again, delighted, "Go to Ayodhyā and govern, Rāma of red-tipped eyes."
38. Then, having made obeisance to the gods, applauded by his friends, he united with his wife like the great Indra with the daughter of Puloman (Indrāṇī).
39. Then the scorcher of enemies (Rāma) granted a boon to Avindhya and furnished the female Rākṣasa Trijaṭā with wealth and honor.
40. Then Brahmā, surrounded by the gods headed by Indra, told him, "Son of Kausalyā, what desired boons shall I grant you today?"
41. Rāma chose constancy in dharma, invincibility by enemies, and the revival of the monkeys struck down by Rākṣasas.
42. Then, O great king (Yudhiṣṭhira), when the word, "So be it," had been spoken by Brahmā, then the monkeys stood up together having regained consciousness.
43. And the fortunate Sītā also granted a boon to Hanūmat, "Your life, son, will be equal to Rāma's fame.
44. And divine enjoyments, made by my grace, will certainly always stand by you, O brown-eyed Hanūmat."
45. Then All the gods headed by Indra disappeared while those of impeccable deeds were watching.
46. But, seeing Rāma united with the daughter of Janaka, Indra's charioteer (Mātali), supremely pleased, said this speech amidst their friends:
47. "O truly brave one, you have removed this sorrow of gods, Gandharvas, and Yakṣas, humans, demons, and serpents.
48. The worlds, the Yakṣas, Rākṣasas, and serpents along with the gods, demons, and Gandharvas, will narrate about you as long as the earth remains."

49. After speaking thus, he requested leave to depart, honored Rāma, best of weapon-bearers, and departed with that chariot which was as brilliant as the sun.
50. Then having placed Sītā before him, Rāma with Sumitrā's son (Lakṣmaṇa), accompanied by all the monkeys headed by Sugrīva, . . .
51. . . . attended by Vibhīṣaṇa, provided protection in Laṅkā and again crossed the abode of sea monsters by that bridge. . .
52. . . . with the beautiful sky-going airship Puṣpaka which moved at will, as a ruler surrounded by his principal ministers.
53. Then on the shore of the sea where the prince had slept, the virtuous one (Rāma) spent the night together with all the monkeys.
54. Then in time the descendant of Raghu (Rāma) brought them together, honored them and sent them away having completely satisfied them with gems.
55. When the monkey-lords and monkeys and bears had gone, Rāma went back again to Kiṣkindhā with Sugrīva. . .
56. . . . followed by Vibhīṣaṇa, showing, in conjunction with Sugrīva, the forest to the princess of Videha with the airship Puṣpaka.
57. After reaching Kiṣkindhā, Rāma, best of attackers, had the accomplished Aṅgada consecrated as crown-prince.
58. Then together with them, Rāma with Sumitrā's son (Lakṣmaṇa) proceeded to his own city by the way he had come.
59. When he reached the city Ayodhyā, the lord of the kingdom (Rāma) dispatched Hanūmat as messenger to Bharata.
60. When the son of the wind (Hanūmat) returned after noticing every gesture and reporting to him (Bharata) the good news, he (Rāma) approached Nandigrāma.
61. There he saw Bharata sitting on a mat with dirt-smeared limbs, wearing bark, having placed (Rāma's) sandals before him.
62. Then, O bull among the descendants of Bharata (Yudhiṣṭhira), the heroic descendant of Raghu (Rāma) with the son of Sumitrā (Lakṣmaṇa) rejoiced upon reuniting with Bharata and Śatrughna.
63. Likewise both Bharata and Śatrughna, upon reuniting then with their elder, became overjoyed at seeing the princess of Videha (Sītā).
64. Filled with supreme joy, Bharata restored his honored trust, the kingdom, to him having come back (Rāma).

65. Then, on an auspicious day under the constellation presided over by Viṣṇu (Śravaṇa), Vasiṣṭha and Vāmadeva together consecrated that hero (Rāma).
66. Having been consecrated, he (Rāma) granted Sugrīva, best of the monkeys, and Vibhīṣaṇa, son of Pulastya, along with the benevolent people, leave to depart to their homes.
67. Having honored with various gems those two (Sugrīva and Vibhīṣaṇa) who were pleased and filled with joy, he accepted his duty and reluctantly let them go.
68. And the descendant of Raghu, delighter of Raghu (Rāma), having honored the airship Puṣpaka, presented it with pleasure to Vaiśravaṇa.
69. After that, in conjunction with gods and seers, he performed ten fiery Aśvamedhas without impediment along the Gomatī river.

Mahābhārata
Āraṇyakaparvan
Adhyāya 276
Mārkaṇḍeya's encouragement of Yudhiṣṭhira

Mārkaṇḍeya said:

1. Thus previously Rāma of unmeasured brilliance suffered this intense misfortune due to living in the forest, O great-armed one (Yudhiṣṭhira).

2. Don't grieve, tiger-like man! You are a kṣatriya, O scorcher of enemies! You are on the path which has as its refuge strength of arms and which requires blazing resolve.

3. For no vice is seen in you, not even a tiny bit. Even the gods and demons including Indra can despair on this path.

4. Vr̥tra was struck down by the thunderbolt-bearer (Indra) after he joined with the Maruts, and so was the unassailable Namuci and the female Rākṣasa Dīrghajīhvā.

5. All aims always attend upon him who has companions here. What is unconquered in battle by him whose brother is the winner of wealth (Arjuna), . . .

6. . . . and this best of the strong, the terrifyingly bold Bhīma, and these two youths, the great archers, twin sons of Mādrī?

7. With these companions who could conquer the army of the thunderbolt-bearer (Indra) along with the troops of Maruts, why do you despair, O scorcher of enemies?

8. You too with these god-like great archers as companions will conquer all enemies in battle, O bull among the descendants of Bharata (Yudhiṣṭhira).
9. And see how just now these great souled ones, by accomplishing a very difficult feat, recovered Kṛṣṇā, the daughter of Drupada, ...
10. ... who had been abducted by the strong, evil-natured king of Sindhu (Jayadratha), mad with virility, and conquered king Jayadratha who came under their control.
11. With companions, Rāma recovered the princess of Videha again after slaying the terrifyingly bold ten-necked Rākṣasa in battle ...
12. ... (Rāma), whose friends were the branch-animals and black-faced bears in different genera. Reflect upon this, O king, with your intellect.
13. Therefore, do not grieve, tiger among the descendants of Kuru, bull among the descendants of Bharata (Yudhiṣṭhira)! For great-souled men like you do not grieve, O scorcher of enemies.

Vaiśaṁpāyana said:
14. Thus reassured by the wise Mārkaṇḍeya, the king (Yudhiṣṭhira) abandoned his sorrow and, undepressed in spirit, said.

Appendices

Glossary of proper names

Agni The god of fire and fire itself, one of the five elements, one of the Vasus (3.260.4), guardian of the south-east, father of the monkey Nīla, messenger of the gods who goes at their head when they approach Brahmā (3.260.1–3), one of those who vouch for Sītā's purity before Rāma after her rescue (3.275.27).

Aṅgada One of the monkey heroes, son of Sugrīva's brother Vālin and Tārā, one of the principal members of the group of monkeys Sugrīva sends south to find Sītā, one of the captains in Sugrīva's army (3.267.19). He trespasses in Sugrīva's honey-forest Madhuvana with Hanūmat upon returning to Kiṣkindhā after Sītā is located (3.266.27), is sent as messenger to Rāvaṇa by Rāma upon arriving in Laṅkā (3.267.54, 3.268.7–22), kills Indrajit's charioteer and destroys his chariot while aiding Lakṣmaṇa in a battle with Indrajit (3.272.14–18), is among those who surround Rāma and Lakṣmaṇa when they are struck down by Indrajit (3.273.4), among those who gain the ability to see the invisible by applying Kubera's water (3.273.13) and those who surround Rāvaṇa when he comes out to fight (3.274.3). He is consecrated as crown-prince upon the return to Kiṣkindhā (3.275.57).

Aja A former ruler of Ayodhyā, son of Raghu and father of Daśaratha in the line of Ikṣvāku.

Ajihvikā One of the female Rākṣasas assigned to guard Sītā near an Aśoka grove within Rāvaṇa's palace (3.264.44).

Aditi Vedic goddess, daughter of Dakṣa, wife of Kaśyapa, mother of the Ādityas and of the gods.

Ayodhyā The capital city of Rāma and other kings of the solar dynasty, built by Manu, the father of Ikṣvāku, described in *Rāmāyaṇa* 1.5, situated on the bank of the Sarayū river in the Kosala district, pre-independence Oude, present day Ayodhyā in Uttar Pradesh.

Aruja One of the Piśāca and Rākṣasa warriors who attack Rāma's troops invisible while they are resting, are exposed by Vibhīṣaṇa, and slain (3.269.1–4).

Aruṇa The dawn personified as the charioteer of the sun, son of Kaśyapa by Vinatā. Kaśyapa, son of Brahmā, married the two daughters of Prajāpati, Kadrū and Vinatā, to whom he granted boons. Kadrū chose to have 1000 serpent sons and Vinatā to have two sons more excellent than Kadrū's sons. Kadrū gave birth to a thousand eggs and Vinatā to two, which they incubated in pots. After five hundred years Kadrū hatched her thousand sons. Jealous, Vinatā broke open one of her eggs. Aruṇa emerged developed only from the waist up, cursed his mother to serve Kadrū until her second son freed her and took his place in the sky as the reddish dawn. After another five hundred years Garuḍa was born from the other egg (*MBh.* 1.14). In female form he bore Vālin to Indra and Sugrīva to the Sun who were raised by Ahalyā, cursed to become monkeys by her husband Gautama, and adopted by Ṛkṣarāja, king of Kiṣkindhā.

Avindhya An aged minister of Rāvaṇa. He advises him to return Sītā to Rāma, sends Sītā an encouraging message by way of Trijaṭā (3.264.55–71), foretells Hanūmat's visit (3.266.64–65), calms and dissuades Rāvaṇa when he undertakes to slay Sītā out of anger after Indrajit's death (273.28–32), accompanies Sītā out of Laṅkā with Vibhīṣaṇa to return her to Rāma after the war (3.275.6–7), and is honored by Rāma (3.275.39).

Aśoka The moderately sized Saraca Indica tree belonging to the leguminous class with smooth gray-brown bark and deep green shiny evergreen foot-long leaves. It gives bloom between January and April to flowers with four oval petals which turn from yellow through orange to crimson, contain long white and crimson stamens, and are fragrant in the night. (Cowen, p. 5.)

Ikṣvāku Son of Manu Vaivasvata, first king in Ayodhyā (*R.* 1.69.19).

Indra The wielder of the thunderbolt and bringer of rain, aided by the Maruts in battle, heroic victor over the obstructor of rain Vṛtra, drought, obstacles and other negative forces including Asuras, Dasyus, Daityas, Dānavas, etc., munificent bestower of success, prosperity, and happiness. In the Ṛgveda he supersedes Varuṇa to become the preeminent Vedic deity, the principal deity summoned to enjoy Vedic performances. He is said to be called Śatakratu because of having performed a hundred Vedic performances though the epithet was applied because he is invoked in numerous Vedic performances. He is lord of the thirty-three (twelve Ādityas, eight Vasus, and eleven Rudras, often rounded to thirty) deities, and king of the gods which he remains even though subordinated in the epics, Purāṇas, and classical Sanskrit literature to Brahmā, Viṣṇu and Śiva. Mālati is his charioteer, Nandana his garden, Vaijayanta, his palace, and Amarāvatī, his city. His wife is Indrāṇī, the daughter of Puloman.

Indrajit Also called Meghanāda 'thunder,' the eldest son of Rāvaṇa by Mandodarī. He performed many Vedic ceremonies and was taught the technique of transcending and the special power of invisibility by Śiva. In the great battle between Indra and Rāvaṇa, he turned invisible, sneaked onto Indra's chariot and bound the god. He was thus named Indrajit by Brahmā, who granted him, in exchange for his father's releasing Indra after a year, the boon that upon completing a Vedic ceremony a chariot would emerge from the fire fighting from which he would not die in battle (*R.* 7.30.8–13). Fights with Lakṣmaṇa during Rāvaṇa's first sortie (3.269.7, 12). Sent out by Rāvaṇa after Kumbhakarṇa's death, he disappears, severely wounds Rāma and Lakṣmaṇa in battle (272.2–26) and binds them with a lattice of arrows (3.273.1). He mounts his invisible chariot after presenting offerings to Agni in a Vedic ceremony (*R.* 6.67.4–10). Returning to battle after their recovery, he is slain by Lakṣmaṇa (3.273.15–24).

Indrāṇī wife of Indra, daughter of Puloman (3.275.38), said to be Śacī because of the interpretation of Indra's Vedic epithet Śacīpati 'lord of strength' as meaning 'husband of Śacī.'

Īśāna A form of Śiva with matted hair riding an ox. See note on 3.265.23.

Uśanas An ancient sage with the patronymic Kāvya identified with Śukra, the teacher of the Asuras, who presides over the planet Venus.

Ṛśyamūka The mountain beside the river Pampā, on top of which Sugrīva and his four associates, Hanūmat, Jāmbavat, etc. are living when the Gandharva Viśvāvasu, who emerged from the slain body of the Rākṣasa Kabandha, recommended that Rāma and Lakṣmaṇa seek his assistance in finding Sītā (3.263.39). *MBhCI.* 1.3, p. 300–301.

Ekapādā One of the female Rākṣasas assigned to guard Sītā near an Aśoka grove within Rāvaṇa's palace (3.264.44).

Ekalocanā One of the female Rākṣasas assigned to guard Sītā near an Aśoka grove within Rāvaṇa's palace (3.264.44).

Kakutstha Purañjaya, son of Vikukṣi/Śaśāda, grandson of Ikṣvāku, father of Anenas, was so called because he rode on the hump of a bull. Requested for assistance in a battle against the demons, he asked that Īndra take the form of a bull to carry him. (*Viṣṇupurāṇa* 4.2.5–12.) He is the son of Bhagīratha and father of Raghu according to *Rāmāyaṇa* 1.69.26.

Kabandha The cask-shaped monster, also called Danu (e.g. *R.* 3.67.18, 24), who seizes Lakṣmaṇa as he and Rāma head south in search of Sītā in Daṇḍaka's forest, has his arms severed, is slain by them, regains the radiant form of the Gandharva Viśvāvasu, and directs them to Sugrīva (3.263.25–43; *R.* 3.67.16–3.70.1). The *Rāmāyaṇa* provides two accounts of how he attained his shape as a cask: 1. He previously had an inconceivable form like the body of the moon, sun, or Indra, but assumed a cask-like shape to frighten sages in the forest. He was cursed to remain in that form until Rāma severed his arms and burnt him in a desolate forest by the great sage Sthūlaśiras whom he angered by tormenting him while he was gathering wild plants. (*R.* 3.67.1–6.) 2. He is the radiant son of Danu (*R.* 3.67.7), who was granted long life by Brahmā on account of his spiritual practice. Indra, when attacked by him, disfigured him by forcing his head and thighs into his body leaving him in the shape of a cask (*kabandha*) but at his plea gave him a mouth in his belly and long arms with which to feed himself and prophesied his release when they were severed by Rāma and Lakṣmaṇa. (*R.* 3.67.8–15.)

Kāma The god of love, son of Dharma ('right, proper function, duty') and husband of Rati ('sexual enjoyment'), whose body is burnt to ashes by Śiva when he attempts to shoot him with his arrow of love while he is absorbed in spiritual practice.

Kāla The Black Mountain in the northwest of the island of Laṅkā.

Kiṁśuka The medium sized Butea frondosa tree ranging from 20 to 40 feet in height, having a crooked trunk and rough, gray bark. It grows large, thick, velvety, bronze-green leaves in April and May which it drops in December and January. Between January and March it covers its crown with a conflagration of scentless five-petaled orange and vermilion flowers from long, velvety, green stalks.

(Cowen, p. 3.)

Kiṣkindhā The monkey city of Vālin and Sugrīva south of Daṇḍaka's forest in southern India.

Kuntī Daughter of a Yādava prince named Śūra who gave her to his childless cousin Kuntibhoja, by whom she was adopted. In return for her extraordinary hospitality to the difficult to please sage Durvāsas, as a girl she obtained a mantra to invoke and have a child by any deity. Before her marriage she invoked the Sun and had a son Karṇa whom she abandoned by setting him afloat in a basket. She was the first wife of Pāṇḍu to whom, after he was cursed to die making love, she bore Yudhiṣṭhira, Bhīmasena and Arjuna by invoking the deities Dharma, Vāyu and Indra respectively. After Pāṇḍu dies and his younger wife Mādrī commits satī, she adopts Mādrī's twins Nakula and Sahadeva, fathered by the Aśvins with the use of her mantra, and brings all five of Pāṇḍus sons back to her husband's city Hāstinapura, where her blind brother-in-law Dhṛtarāṣṭra rules.

Kubera The god of wealth, regent of the northern quarter, chief of the Yakṣas, a friend of Rudra, owner of the airship Puṣpaka, represented as having three legs and only eight teeth, son of Pulastya (later called Viśravas) by Go or, according to the *Viṣṇupurāṇa* and *Bhāgavatapurāṇa*, Iḍaviḍā, daughter of Tṛṇabindu. He was originally made lord of the Rākṣasas in Laṅkā. When he is driven out by Rāvaṇa he settles on Mount Gandhamādana. He is usually called by the patronymic Vaiśravaṇa 'son of Viśravan.' 'Viśravan' synonymous with 'Viśravas,' refers to Pulastya's reincarnation of half of himself (3.258.14).

Kumuda One of the monkey heroes in Sugrīva's army who surrounds Rāma and Lakṣmaṇa when they fall struck by Indrajit's arrows (3.273.4).

Kumbhakarṇa Rāvaṇa's giant brother, son of Viśravas by Puṣpotkaṭā, who chooses sleep when granted a boon by Brahmā for his spiritual practice (3.259.28). About to devour Sugrīva in the war at Laṅkā, he is slain by Lakṣmaṇa with Brahmā's weapon (3.271.16).

Kuru Son of Saṁvaraṇa and Tapatī (daughter of the sun), ancestor of the Kurus including Yudhiṣṭhira and his brothers.

Kṛṣṇā The daughter of Drupada, hence called Draupadī, sister of Dhṛṣṭadyumna, and the princess of Pāñcāla, hence called Pāñcālī, won by Arjuna at her svayaṁvara to become the common wife of the five sons of Pāṇḍu, i.e. Yudhiṣṭhira, Bhīma, Arjuna, Nakula, and Sahadeva. Saved by miracle from being publicly disrobed at the court of Hāstinapura when Yudhiṣṭhira looses her gambling at dice, she is granted freedom for herself and her husbands by king Dhṛtarāṣṭra. She accompanies her husbands to the forest in their exile, where she is abducted by Jayadratha while they are out hunting. It is just after her recovery that Yudhiṣṭhira asks Mārkaṇḍeya the question that prompts the narration of the *Rāmopākhyāna*. The later *Bhāgavatapurāṇa* makes another link to the *Rāmāyaṇa* through her by narrating that she is the reincarnation of a shadow Sītā who is set in the real Sītā's place before Rāvaṇa abducts her and remains there until Agni restores the real Sītā after the fall of Laṅkā. The shadow Sītā gains reincarnation as Kṛṣṇā after years of spiritual practice in Puṣkara in answer to her five-times repeated request of Śiva to have a husband.

Kaikeyī Daughter of a king of the Kekayas, sister of Yudhājit, one of the wives of Daśaratha and mother of Bharata (3.258.8), who in claiming a boon previously promised her by her husband wishes that her son be consecrated crown prince instead of Rāma and that Rāma be sent to the forest (3.261.16–25), recalls her son after Rāma's departure and Daśaratha's death, advises him to seize the kingdom, is rebuked by him (3.261.30–33), and brought along on the journey to Citrakūṭa to recall Rāma (3.261.35).

Kosala The country on the banks of the Sarayū river having Ayodhyā as its capital, named for the Kṣatriyas, the descendants of Māthavya Videgha, inhabiting it.

Kausalyā Princess of Kosala, wife of Daśaratha, mother of Rāma (3.258.8). She accompanies Bharata on his journey to Citrakūṭa to recall Rāma to Ayodhyā (3.261.35).

Krātha One of the leaders in Sugrīva's monkey army (3.267.19).

Krodhavaśa One of the Piśāca and Rākṣasa warriors who attacks Rāma's army invisible while they are resting (3.269.2–4), are recognized and made visible by Vibhīṣaṇa, and slain by the monkeys.

Khara Rāvaṇa's younger brother, son of Viśravas and Rākā, who with his twin sister Śūrpaṇakhā (3.259.8), serve his elder brothers Rāvaṇa, Kumbhakarṇa and Vibhīṣaṇa when they perform spiritual practice (3.259.19). He and fourteen thousand Rākṣasas in Janasthāna are slain by Rāma (3.261.43).

Khara[2] One of the Piśāca and Rākṣasa warriors who attack Rāma's army invisible while they are resting (3.269.2–4), are recognized and made visible by Vibhīṣaṇa, and slain by the monkeys.

Gaja A monkey general in Sugrīva's army who commands a billion soldiers (3.267.3).

Gandhamādana A mountain in the Himalayan range east of Meru forming the division between Ilāvṛta and Bhadrāśva, named for its fragrant forests. Home of Viśravas and his children (3.259.13) and the place where Vaiśravaṇa takes refuge after Rāvaṇa drives him out of Laṅkā (3.259.33). Home of Sugrīva's general called Gandhamādana (3.267.5). *MBhCI.* 1.3, p. 342–345.

Gandhamādana[2] A monkey-general in Sugrīva's army who commands ten billion soldiers (3.267.5), son of Kubera (*R.* 1.16.491*5).

Garuḍa King of the birds, vehicle of Viṣṇu, son of Kaśyapa and Vinatā, brother of Aruṇa who is the charioteer of the sun.

Gavaya A monkey general in Sugrīva's army who commands a billion soldiers (3.267.3), son of Vaivasvata.

Gavākṣa A monkey general in Sugrīva's army who commands six hundred billion soldiers (3.267.4), son of Vaivasvata and leader of the Golāṅgulas. He is devoured by Kumbhakarṇa in the battle at Laṅkā (3.271.4).

Go Wife of Pulastya and mother of Vaiśravaṇa (3.258.12), who according to the *Viṣṇupurāṇa* and *Bhāgavatapurāṇa* is Iḍaviḍā, daughter of Tṛṇabindu.

Gokarṇa A place of pilgrimage on the Malabar coast, at the northern extremity of Kerala, sacred to Śiva.

Godāvarī A river in the Deccan beside which Rāma and Lakṣmaṇa stay in Daṇḍaka's forest (3.261.40). It flows from Brahmagiri, near Tryambakajyotirliṅga of present-day Nasik northeast of Mumbai east through Rajahmundry and empties into the Bay of Bengal. *MBhCI.* 1.3, p. 348–349.

Gomatī A river in northeastern India, described as having along its banks the Naimiṣa forest and Nāgapura, along the bank of which Rāma performs ten Aśvamedha ceremonies after his return to Ayodhyā (3.275.69). It originates just south of the western end of present day Nepal and flows through Lucknow in Uttar Pradesh emptying into the Ganges north of and downstream from Vārāṇasī. *MBhCI.* 1.3, p.

349–350.

Citrakūṭa The hill and district Citrakote on the Paisuni river, a small southern tributary to the Yamuna, about fifty miles southeast of Banda on the border of Madhya Pradesh in southern Uttar Pradesh. First habitation of the exiled Rāma, Lakṣmaṇa and Sītā, where Bharata approaches him to request his return to Ayodhyā (3.261.37), and where, as Sītā narrates to Hanūmat in 3.266.67, Rāma cast an arrow at a crow molesting Sītā. It remains crowded with temples as the holiest spot of Rāma's worshippers. *MBhCI.* 1.3, p. 353.

Jaṭāyus King of the vultures, son of Aruṇa and Śyenī, younger brother of Saṁpāti, friend of Daśaratha's, who is slain attempting to prevent Rāvaṇa from abducting Sītā (3.262.41–263.6). *MBhCI.* 1.1, p. 22–23. Lineage: *R.* 3.13.6–33.

Janaka Father of Sītā (3.258.9), also called Sīradhvaja 'he whose banner is a plow.' He discovered Sītā in a furrow while plowing his fields (*R.* 1.65.14). He is king of Videha with its capital at Mithilā, son of Hrasvaroman, descendant of Ikṣvāku through his youngest son Nimi who founded the kingdom of Videha and his son Mithi who founded the city Mithilā. Lineage: *R.* 1.70.1–13.

Janamejaya The king to whom Vaiśaṁpāyana relates the *Mahābhārata* in the intervals of his great snake rite. He is the son of Parikṣit, grandson of Abhimanyu, and great-grandson of Arjuna, the third of the five Pāṇḍavas who are the principal figures in the *Mahābhārata.* In response to his request to Vyāsa, who arrives at his snake rite with his students, to tell him about the deeds of his ancestors, Vyāsa asks his principal disciple Vaiśaṁpāyana to narrate the epic (*MBh.* 1.54). Janamejaya undertook the snake rite for the purpose of destroying all snakes after learning that his father died by being bitten by the venomous serpent Takṣaka (*MBh.* 1.46.34–1.47.9) but he halted the rite prior to its completion (*MBh.* 1.51.16–23).

Janasthāna Literally, 'place of people,' the part of the Daṇḍaka forest in which Khara lives (3.261.41).

Jambha One of the Piśāca and Rākṣasa warriors who attack Rāma's troops invisible while they are resting, are exposed by Vibhīṣaṇa, and slain (3.269.1–4).

Jayadratha The king of Sindhu and Sauvīra, one of the kings who fail to win Kṛṣṇā at her svayaṁvara, who abducts Kṛṣṇā, the wife of the Pāṇḍavas, from their forest hermitage while they are out hunting. His army is overtaken and defeated by the Pāṇḍavas and his head is shaved by Bhīma (3.257.7, 3.276.10). But he is released by Yudhiṣṭhira. He later fights with the Kauravas against the Pāṇḍavas.

Jāmbavat The bear-king who is one of Sugrīva's four counselors (3.264.23) and general of an army of a billion streak-faced black bears (3.267.8). He accompanies Lakṣmaṇa when he pierces the southern gate of Laṅkā (3.268.24), is among those who gain the ability to see the invisible Rākṣasas by applying the water sent by Vaiśravaṇa (3.273.13), and those who surround Rāvaṇa when he comes out to fight (3.274.3). He is the son of Brahmā and father of Jāmbavatī whom Kr̥ṣṇa marries.

Tāra One of Sugrīva's monkey-generals, son of Br̥haspati (*R.* 1.16.491*3). He fights against Nikharvaṭa (3.269.8), is among those who encounter Kumbhakarṇa (3.271.5–6) when he emerges to fight and those who surround Rāma and Lakṣmaṇa when Indrajit binds them with lattices of arrows (3.273.4).

Tārā A female monkey, daughter of Suṣeṇa, wife of Vālin and mother of Aṅgada. She was taken as wife by Sugrīva when he presumed that Vālin was slain by Māyāvin (*R.* 4.45.8) but Vālin took her from him when he slew Māyāvin and escaped the cave (*R.* 4.8.32). She tries to dissuade Vālin from going out to meet Sugrīva's challenge (3.264.16–21). After Vālin's death she is taken again as wife by Sugrīva (3.264.39).

Tuṇḍa A Rākṣasa who fights against Nala in the battle at Laṅkā (3.269.8).

Trikūṭa A mountain in Śrīlaṅkā on top of which the city Laṅkā is situated (*R.* 6.30.20).

Trijaṭā One of the female Rākṣasas assigned to guard Sītā near an Aśoka grove within Rāvaṇa's palace (3.264.44). She consoles Sītā (3.264.53–72) and is honored for it by Rāma after the fall of Laṅkā (3.275.39).

Tristanī One of the female Rākṣasas assigned to guard Sītā near an Aśoka grove within Rāvaṇa's palace (3.264.44).

Tryakṣī One of the female Rākṣasas assigned to guard Sītā near an Aśoka grove within Rāvaṇa's palace (3.264.44).

Tvaṣṭr̥ Viśvakarman (q.v.) (3.267.41); Brahmā (3.258.9).

Daṇḍaka The youngest son of Ikṣvāku after whom the Daṇḍakāraṇya is said to be named, reincarnation of Krodhahantr̥ (*MBh.* 1.61.43).

Daṇḍaka's forest The great forest through which the Godāvarī river flows in south India (3.261.40), where Śarabhaṅga's hermitage is located, where Rāma, Sītā, and Lakṣmaṇa dwell after leaving Citrakūṭa during their exile (3.261.39), where Rāma slays Rāvaṇa's brother Khara, his general Dūṣaṇa (3.261.43), and fourteen thousand Rākṣasas (3.261.42) and Rāma and Lakṣmaṇa encounter Kabandha (3.263.23–43). It originated from the burning of Daṇḍaka's kingdom between the Vindhya and Śaivala mountains by Indra at the request of the sage Uśanas after Daṇḍaka raped his daughter Arajā (*R.* 7.70.14–72.21). *MBhCI.* 1.3, pp. 360–361.

Dadhimukha An elder monkey general (3.267.7), son of the moon (*R.*6.21.22), maternal uncle of Sugrīva and guardian of Sugrīva's honey forest Madhuvana (*R.* 5.59.9).

Danu Daughter of Dakṣa, one of Kaśyapa's wives, mother of the demons called Dānavas numbering 40 or 100. Adoptive mother of Vr̥tra. (*Śatapathabrāhmaṇa* 1.6.3.9.)

Dardura A mountain in southern India. *MBhCI.* 1.3, p. 361.

Daśaratha Father of Rāma, Lakṣmaṇa, Bharata, and Śatrughna (3.258.7); son of Aja in the line of Ikṣvāku (3.258.6); husband of Kausalyā, Kaikeyī, and Sumitrā (3.258.8), and virtuous king of Ayodhyā (3.261.3). Prepared to consecrate Rāma king (3.261.13–15), he is requested by his wife Kaikeyī to grant a previously promised boon, which he does (3.261.21–22). He remains silent when she asks that her son Bharata be made king instead of Rāma and that Rāma be banished to the forest (3.261.25–26) but dies from grief (3.261.29) upon Rāma, Sītā, and Lakṣmaṇa's departure. He appears in a divine, radiant form in a lustrous vehicle yoked with geese (3.275.19) when Rāma initially rejects Sītā when she is led out to him from Laṅkā after the defeat of Rāvaṇa. He approves of him accepting her back and bids him return to rule Ayodhyā (3.275.35).

Diti Daughter of Dakṣa, wife of Kaśyapa, and mother of the Daityas, a class of demons.

Dīrghajīhvā One of the female Rākṣasas assigned to guard Sītā near an Aśoka grove within Rāvaṇa's palace (3.264.44).

Dundubhī The female Gandharva who incarnates as Mantharā, Kaikeyī's hunch-backed maid-servant, at Brahmā's bidding to help accomplish the purpose of the gods (3.260.9–10).

Dūṣaṇa A Rākṣasa general, elder brother of Vajravega and Pramāthin, slain by Rāma in Daṇḍaka's forest (3.261.43).

Drupada Also called Yajñasena, son of Somaka, king of the Pañcālas; father of Kṛṣṇā, wife of the five Pāṇḍavas, who is thus given the patronymic Draupadī. After he becomes king, he rejects his childhood friend Droṇa who in revenge, after becoming the teacher of the Pāṇḍavas at Hāstinapura, has them conquer his kingdom, the southern half of which Droṇa keeps for his own and the northern half of which he returns to him. To acquire a son to get revenge, Drupada performs a ceremony from the fire of which arises his son Dhṛṣṭadyumna and daughter Kṛṣṇā. The Pāṇḍavas win the latter at her svayaṁvara and stay with Drupada for a year after their marriage to her. Drupada fights on their side in the war between the Pāṇḍavas and the Kurus, is slain by Droṇa, but avenged by his son Dhṛṣṭadyumna who slays Droṇa.

Dvivida One of Sugrīva's four ministers (3.264.23) and generals (3.267.19) in the army allied with Rāma, said to be progenerated by the Aśvins (*R.* 1.16.491*9–10). He was among those who surround Rāma and Lakṣmaṇa when they are struck down by Indrajit (3.273.4) and those who gain the ability to see the invisible Rākṣasas by applying the water sent by Vaiśravaṇa (3.273.13).

Dvyakṣī One of the female Rākṣasas assigned to guard Sītā near an Aśoka grove within Rāvaṇa's palace (3.264.44).

Dharma The personification of dharma, identified in the Mahābhārata with Yama, the god of death. He fathered Yudhiṣṭhira on Kuntī.

Dhūmrākṣa A Rākṣasa general slain by Hanūmat (3.270.14).

Nandana Indra's divine garden.

Nandigrāma A village near Daulat-ābād from which Bharata administers the kingdom during Rāma's banishment (3.261.38) in sympathetic self-banishment. He rules in Rāma's name keeping Rāma's sandals before him (3.275.60–61).

Namuci A demon slain by Indra (Ṛgveda 8.14.13).

Nala The monkey-chief (3.267.19), son of Tvaṣṭṛ or Viśvakarman (3.267.41, *R.* 1.16.491*6), who constructs the floating causeway from

Rāmeśvara to Śrīlaṅkā for the army of monkeys to pass (3.267.42–45). He fights with the Rākṣasa Tuṇḍa at Laṅkā, is among those who surround Rāma and Lakṣmaṇa when they are struck down by Indrajit (3.273.4) and those who surround Rāvaṇa when he comes out to fight (3.274.3).

Nalakūbara The son of Vaiśravaṇa (3.258.16), cursed his uncle Rāvaṇa after he raped his wife that his head would split into seven pieces if he should ever again approach another woman against her will (3.264.58–59; *R.* 7.26.23–24, 42–44).

Nikharvaṭa A Rākṣasa who fights with the monkey Tāra in the war at Laṅkā (3.269.8).

Nirṛti Goddess of death and corruption often associated with the god of death Mṛtyu and the goddess of illiberality Arāti. She is regarded as the mother of fear, terror, death, and hell and as the daughter of vice and violence, or as the wife of vice. She binds mortals with her cords. She is regent of the south or southwest and of the asterism Mūlā.

Nīla A monkey-chief, son of Agni (*R.* 1.16.491*7), sent south in search of Sītā (*R.* 4.40.1–2), a general of Sugrīva's army (3.267.19), who slays the Rākṣasa Pramāthin at Laṅkā (3.271.25), is among those who surround Rāma and Lakṣmaṇa when they are struck down by Indrajit (3.273.4), those who gain the ability to see the invisible Rākṣasas by applying the water sent by Vaiśravaṇa (3.273.13), and those who surround Rāvaṇa when he comes out to fight (3.274.3).

Paṭuśa A Rākṣasa who fights against the monkey Panasa in the battle at Laṅkā (3.269.8).

Panasa A monkey general contributing five hundred and seventy million monkeys to Sugrīva's army (3.267.6). He fights against the Rākṣasa Paṭuśa in the battle at Laṅkā (3.269.8) and is devoured by Kumbhakarṇa (3.271.4).

Pampā A river in south India flowing near Mount Ṛśyamūka (3.263.4o) where Rāma laments Sītā's loss (3.264.3) and worships the water and his ancestors (3.264.8).

Parvaṇa One of the Piśāca and Rākṣasa warriors who attack Rāma's troops invisible while they are resting, are exposed by Vibhīṣaṇa, and slain (3.269.1–4).

Pāṇḍu King of Hāstinapura, son of Vicitravīrya, younger brother of

Dhṛtarāṣṭra, husband of Kuntī and Mādrī, who abandons his throne to live in the forest. He is the legal father of Yudhiṣṭhira, Bhīma, Arjuna, Nakula, and Sahadeva.

Pulastya The mind-born son of Prajāpati (Brahmā 3.259.35), husband of Go, and father of Vaiśravaṇa (3.258.12), who, when his son abandons him for his grandfather Prajāpati, takes birth with half of his body as Viśravas (3.258.14, 3.259.1), in which form he fathers Rāvaṇa, Vibhīṣaṇa, and their other siblings (3.259.6–8).

Puloman A demon, son of Danu (*MBh.* 1.59.21–22), father of Śacī, Indra's wife (*Matsyapurāṇa* 6.21). Taking the form of a boar, he carried off Pulomā, the pregnant wife of Bhṛgu who had previously been promised to him, but was turned to ashes at the sight of Cyavana who fell prematurely from Pulomā's womb (*MBh.* 1.5–6). He was slain by Indra when about to curse him for taking his daughter (Sharma vol. 2, p. 270, note 2).

Puṣpaka The self-moving aerial car made by Viśvakarman from the luminous dust produced from rubbing the Sun, his son-in-law, on a grindstone in an attempt to dim his brightness which his daughter could not bear. Viśvakarman gave it to Brahmā who gave it to Kubera after his long spiritual practice. It is carried off by the demon Rāvaṇa when he drives Kubera out of Laṅkā (3.259.34). Kubera vows that it will not carry Rāvaṇa but will carry his slayer (3.259.34–35). After Rāma slays Rāvaṇa he employs the car to transport himself and Sītā back to Ayodhyā via Kiṣkindhā (3.275.52, 56) before he returns it to Kubera (3.275.68).

Puṣpotkaṭā One of the three female Rākṣasas Vaiśravaṇa gives Viśravas to appease him, mother of Rāvaṇa and Kumbhakarṇa (3.259.3–7).

Pūtana One of the Piśāca and Rākṣasa warriors who attack Rāma's troops invisible while they are resting, are exposed by Vibhīṣaṇa, and slain (3.269.1–4).

Praghasa One of the Piśāca and Rākṣasa warriors who attack Rāma's troops invisible while they are resting, are exposed by Vibhīṣaṇa, and slain (3.269.1–4).

Prajāpati Brahmā, the self-existent creator of the worlds (3.258.11), father of Pulastya, grandfather of Kubera and of Rāvaṇa and his siblings.

Prabhāvatī A female spiritual practitioner who is performing spiritual practice at the abode of the demon architect Maya.

Pramāthin A Rākṣasa, one of the younger brothers of Dūṣaṇa, the other being Vajravega, who accompany Kumbhakarṇa out to battle (3.270.27) and are apprehended by Lakṣmaṇa (3.271.20). He is slain by Nīla (3.271.25).

Praruja One of the Piśāca and Rākṣasa warriors who attack Rāma's troops invisible while they are resting, are exposed by Vibhīṣaṇa, and slain (3.269.1–4).

Prahasta Rāvaṇa's chief minister, slain by Vibhīṣaṇa in battle at Laṅkā (3.270.1–5).

Prahlāda A pious Daitya, son of Hiraṇyakaśipu (*Matsyapurāṇa* 6.8–9) and Kayādhū, made king of the Daityas by Viṣṇu after killing Hiraṇyakaśipu in the form of Narasiṁha.

Bṛhaspati Lord of speech, the teacher, spiritual advisor, and performer of ceremonies for the gods. He is the god of wisdom and eloquence, regarded as son of Aṅgiras, husband of Tārā, and father of Kaca. In astronomy he is the regent of Jupiter and often identified with that planet.

Brahmā Properly *brahmán* (masculine), the self-existent absolute, eternal spirit, manifested as a personal Creator distinguished from *bráhman* (neuter), the one unmanifest impersonal self-existent absolute eternal spirit, universal soul or divine essence and source from which all created things emanate, with which they are identified, and to which they return.

Bharata A quarter-part incarnation of Viṣṇu (*R.* 1.17.8), son of Daśaratha and Kaikeyī and younger brother of Rāma (3.258.7–8). His half-brother Śatrughna is his devoted companion as Lakṣmaṇa is to Rāma. At the time of Rāma's marriage to Sītā, he marries Māṇḍavī, daughter of Kuśadhvaja, Janaka's younger brother (*R.* 1.72.19). He and Śatrughna go to visit his mother's homeland, Kekaya, with his maternal uncle and the country's king, Yudhājit (*R.* 2.1.2–3). The coronation of Rāma is arranged in his absence (*R.* 2.4.25–27). After his mother removes the impediments to him becoming king by requesting that he be consecrated instead of Rāma and that Rāma be exiled (3.261.25), and after the death of his father from grief upon Rāma's departure (3.261.29), messengers request his return (*R.* 2.62.2–

3). He rebukes his mother for causing the death of his father and the exile of Rāma and refuses to accept rulership (3.261.32–33). Instead he goes after Rāma to bring him back (3.261.34), and upon his refusal, administers the kingdom in his name, living the life of an ascetic in Nandigrāma until his return (3.261.38, 3.275.61) for which he is remembered as the embodiment of virtue and of brotherly trust and devotion. As his uncle Yudhājit's general (*R.* 7.91.1), he conquers the land of the Gandharvas (Gāndhāra) and installs his two sons as kings in them, Takṣa in Takṣaśilā and Puṣkala in Puṣkalāvati (*R.* 7.91.9). He Declines to succeed to the throne of Ayodhyā at Rāma's retirement in favor of Rāma's sons Lava and Kuśa (*R.* 7.97.5–7). He accompanies Rāma in his renunciation (*R.* 7.99.11).

Bharata[2] Son of Duḥṣanta and Śakuntalā, ancient emperor of northern India, who through his son Bhūmanyu, whom he obtained from Bharadvāja, became ancestor of Saṁtanu and most of the figures in the Mahābhārata (*MBh.* 1.89.16–19).

Bhīma The second son of Pāṇḍu and Kuntī, fathered by Vāyu, the wind.

Madhumādhavī alcohol or specifically the liquor of the Michelia Campaka tree.

Madhuvana The honey-forest protected by the monkey kings Vālin and Sugrīva and enjoyed by Hanūmat, Aṅgada, and the other monkeys who search the south for Sītā (3.266.26–27).

Mantharā Kaikeyī's hunch-backed maid-servant, the incarnation of the female Gandharva Dundubhī (3.260.10), who advises Kaikeyī of impending misfortune upon learning that the king is preparing to consecrate Kausalyā's son Rāma crown-prince (3.261.16–18). She thereby incites her to intervene to get her own son Bharata consecrated.

Mandodarī Rāvaṇa's queen, favorite wife, daughter of Maya and the apsaras Hemā (*R.* 7.12.16), and mother of Indrajit (3.265.16).

Maya The architect of the Daityas, son of Diti, whose abode the monkeys searching the south for Sītā visit (3.266.40). He gives his daughter Mandodarī as bride to Rāvaṇa (*R.* 7.12.15–17). Saved from the fire devouring the Khāṇḍava forest (*MBh.* 1.219.35–40), he builds the palace of the Pāṇḍavas in Indraprastha (*MBh.* 2.2–3).

Marīci One of the Prajāpatis (*R.* 3.13.8) and ancestor of Mārīca, one of the seven ṛṣis.

Maruts The storm-gods, Indra's companions, the sons of Rudra and Pṛśni, or the children of heaven or of ocean, armed with golden weapons, i.e. lightnings and thunderbolts, having iron teeth, roaring like lions, residing in the north, riding in golden cars drawn by ruddy horses sometimes called Pṛṣatīḥ (*Ṛgveda*). They are among the gods of the middle sphere (*Naighaṇṭu* 5.5) and are numbered three times sixty (RV. 8.96.8). In the later literature they are the children of Diti, numbered either seven or seven times seven, and are sometimes said to be led by Mātariśvan (MW).

Malaya A mountain range on the west of Malabar, the western Ghāts, abounding in Sandal trees (MW), on the southern sea near Mounts Sahya and Dardura (3.266.42–43). *MBhCI.* 1.4, p. 407.

Mātali Indra's charioteer who offers Indra's chariot and his services to Rāma in his final battle with Rāvaṇa (3.274.12–14, *R.* 6.90.4–12, *R.* 6.97.1–3), praises his feat, and departs (3.275.46–49, *R.* 6.100.4–6).

Mādrī Princess of the Madras, second wife of Pāṇḍu, mother of the twins Nakula and Sahadeva.

Mādhvīka Liquor made from the flowers of the Madhupuṣpa, the tree called Bassia Latifolia or Madhuca Indica (Cowen, pp. 73–75).

Mārīca Descendant of Marīci, the Yakṣa son of Tāṭakā and Sunda (*R.* 1.23.25), who, after being turned into a Rākṣasa by Agastya (*R.* 1.24.8–10), serves as Rāvaṇa's minister and terrorizes the forest with Subāhu (*R.* 1.19.24–25). Wounded by the youthful Rāma when he interferes with Viśvāmitra's Vedic performance (*R.* 1.29.11–17), he resorts to the life of a spiritual practitioner in Gokarṇa out of fear of Rāma (3.261.54–55, 3.262.6–7, *R.* 3.37). He is coerced by Rāvaṇa into helping him abduct Sītā (3.262.8–10) which he does by taking the form of a bejeweled deer, enticing Sītā to send Rāma after him, drawing Rāma far from the hermitage, and crying for help in Rāma's voice to induce Sītā to send Lakṣmaṇa after him (3.262.11–12, 17–22).

Mārkaṇḍeya The age-old sage, descendant of Mṛkaṇḍu, who narrates the stories of Rāma and of Sāvitrī (3.257.1–3.283.16) to Yudhiṣṭhira in the Kāmyaka forest after the abduction and recapture of his wife Kṛṣṇā after having previously answered many questions and told him many other stories (*MBh.* 3.180.39–3.222.80). Narrator of the *Mārkaṇḍeyapurāṇa.*

Mālyavat The mountain near which Sugrīva is standing when Vālin emerges from his cave to meet his challenge (3.264.26) and upon which Rāma and Lakṣmaṇa dwelt for four months while the monkeys searched for Sītā (3.264.40, 3.266.1, 21).

Mithilā The capital city of Videha, modern Tirhut in northeast India, in which Sītā's father Janaka rules. Said to be founded by his ancestor Mithi. Present-day Mithilā lies north of Patna near the Nepal border.

Mṛkaṇḍu A sage, ancestor of Mārkaṇḍeya.

Mālinī One of the three female Rākṣasas Vaiśravaṇa gives Viśravas to appease him (3.259.3–5), mother of Vibhīṣaṇa (3.259.8).

Mṛgaśīrṣa The Nakṣatra Mṛgaśiras containing three stars in the shape of a deer's head.

Mainda One of Sugrīva's four ministers (3.264.23) and generals (3.267.19) in the army allied with Rāma, said to be progenerated by the Aśvins (*R.* 1.16.491*9–10). He is among those who surround Rāma and Lakṣmaṇa when they are struck down by Indrajit (3.273.4), those who gain the ability to see the invisible Rākṣasas by applying the water sent by Vaiśravaṇa (3.273.13), and those who surround Rāvaṇa when he comes out to fight (3.274.3).

Yama The god of death, son of the Sun and Saraṇyū, twin brother of Yamī, regent of the South, who as the judge of the dead is called *dharmarāja*.

Yudhiṣṭhira The eldest of the five recognized sons of Pāṇḍu, son of Kuntī, Pāṇḍu's first wife, fathered by the god Dharma, dharma personified, who is identified in the Mahābhārata with Yama, the god of death. Therefore, Yudhiṣṭhira is often called *dharmaputra* or *dharmarāja*. After reigning in Indraprastha, he is defeated at dice by his cousin Duryodhana, lives in exile with his brothers and wife for twelve years and in hiding for a thirteenth year, defeats the Kurus in battle when Duryodhana refuses to return his kingdom in accordance with the agreement of the dice-match, rules at Hāstinapura.

Raghu Rāma's great-grandfather, grandfather of Daśaratha, father of Aja, the son of Kakutstha (*R.* 1.69.26) or the son of Dilīpa and Sudakṣiṇā (*Raghuvaṁśa* 3.13–21).

Rambhā An Apsaras, wife of Nalakūbara, carried off by Rāvaṇa

(3.264.59), sometimes regarded as a form of Lakṣmī and as the most beautiful woman of Indra's paradise. (MW)

Rākā One of the three female Rākṣasas Vaiśravaṇa gave Viśravas to appease him (3.259.3–5), mother of Khara and Śūrpaṇakhā (3.259.8).

Rāma The incarnation of Viṣṇu (3.260.5), a half-part incarnation of Viṣṇu (*R.* 1.17.6), identified with Viṣṇu (*R.* 6.105.14, 25), son of Daśaratha and Kausalyā and eldest of four half brothers (3.258.7–8, 3.261.6). He wins Sītā's hand when he lifts Śiva's bow (*R.* 1.65.27, *R.* 1.66.16–17, 22–23) and Janaka gives her to him in marriage and his other daughter and nieces to his brothers (*R.* 1.72.17–20). He voluntarily sets out for the forest to preserve his father's truthfulness (3.261.27) when he learns that Kaikeyī requested as a boon granted by his father, on the verge of his consecration as crown prince (3.261.8–15), that her son Bharata be consecrated instead of him and that he be exiled (3.261.25). His half brother Lakṣmaṇa and wife Sītā accompany him (3.261.28). His father dies of sorrow upon his departure (3.261.29) and Bharata accompanied by his father's wives, ministers, and all the citizens approach him in Citrakūṭa to request him to return to rule Ayodhyā (3.261.34–37). He refuses, insisting upon carrying out the word of his father (3.261.38) and after sending them away proceeds south by way of Śarabhaṅga's hermitage (3.261.39) to Daṇḍaka's forest where he dwells with Sītā and Lakṣmaṇa on the bank of the Godāvarī River (3.261.40). There he slays fourteen thousand Rākṣasas (3.261.42), including Rāvaṇa's brother Khara (3.261.43), and causes Rāvaṇa's sister Śūrpaṇakhā to be disfigured (3.261.44–45, *R.* 3.17.20–21). His wife Sītā is then abducted by Rāvaṇa while he and Lakṣmaṇa are drawn away from the hermitage (3.262.16–40). He learns from Jaṭāyus, the vulture slain defending her, that Rāvaṇa abducted her and heads south (3.263.20–21). He is directed to Sugrīva on Mount Ṛśyamūka by the Gandharva Viśvāvasu who emerges from the slain body of the Ṛākṣasa Kabandha (3.262.38–42). He laments the loss of his beloved at the river Pampā (3.264.1–3). He enters into a treaty with Sugrīva to slay his brother Vālin and install him as king in Kiṣkindhā in exchange for Sugrīva's help in finding and recovering Sītā (3.264.11–14, 21). He slays Vālin while Vālin is battling with Sugrīva for which he is rebuked by the dying victim (3.264.35–38). After several months dwelling on

Mount Mālyavat (3.264.40), he hears of Sītā's whereabouts from Hanūmat (3.266.36, 68). He proceeds south with an army of monkeys (3.267.15) to the ocean (3.267.21) whom he implores and threatens to make a way for the army to pass to Laṅkā (3.267.30–37). Upon the ocean's advice (3.267.41) he asks Nala to build a bridge (3.267.43). He welcomes Rāvaṇa's brother Vibhīṣaṇa, makes him his counselor, and consecrates him to kingship over the Rākṣasas (3.267.46–49). He traverses the ocean with the army (3.267.50), sets up camp in the forest, dispatches Aṅgada as emissary to Rāvaṇa (3.267.54–268.1), begins the assault on Laṅkā (3.268.23), and encounters Rāvaṇa in battle (3.269.6–7). He is brought down by Rāvaṇa's son Indrajit fighting invisible (3.272.21–26), but is restored to consciousness by Vibhīṣaṇa (3.273.5), healed by Sugrīva (3.273.6), and attains the power to see creatures who have disappeared (3.273.9–14). Mounts Indra's chariot, engages Rāvaṇa in battle (3.274.17), and slays him with Brahmā's weapon (3.274.24–30). After being honored by the gods (3.275.2), he presents Laṅkā to Vibhīṣaṇa (3.275.5). He initially rejects Sītā (3.275.10–13) but accepts her back (3.275.38) when Brahmā, Vāyu, Agni, Varuṇa, and his father (3.275.17–35) vouch for her purity and urge him to do so. In the Rāmāyaṇa, Agni restores her to him (*R.* 6.106.3–9) and he accepts her (*R.* 6.106.10–20). He rewards Rāvaṇa's father-in-law Avindhya and Trijaṭā, the female Rākṣasa who reassured Sītā, (3.275.39) and is himself granted a boon by Brahmā, which he uses to revive the slain monkeys (3.275.40–41). He returns, on the aerial car Puṣpaka, which he then restores to its rightful owner Kubera (3.275.68), to Kiṣkindhā, where he has Vālin's son Aṅgada consecrated as crown prince (3.275.57), and thence to Ayodhyā with Sītā and Lakṣmaṇa, where Bharata, who administered the kingdom in his name living the life of an ascetic in Nandigrāma until his return (3.261.38, 3.275.61), restores the kingdom to him. He performs ten Aśvamedhas along the Gomatī river (3.275.69). He banishes Sītā (*R.* 7.44.15) out of concern for public opinion (*R.* 7.88.3, *R.* 7.87.14–15, 20) because of complaints about the example he set by accepting her back (*R.* 7.42.16–19) but seeks reconciliation with her (*R.* 7.86.4–6, *R.* 7.88.4) after he recognizes (*R.* 7.86.2) and is introduced to his sons Kuśa and Lava (*R.*7.58.1–6, *R.* 7.87.16) when they have completed their recitation of the *Rāmāyaṇa* (*R.* 7.86.2). He installs Lakṣmaṇa's sons Aṅgada and Candraketu in Kārupatha and Candrakānta (*R.* 7.92.6). After a long rule he announces his intention to retire to the forest (*R.* 7.97.2), leaves his kingdom to his sons Kuśa and Lava (*R.* 7.97.17–18), and reenters the realm of Viṣṇu (*R.* 7.100.10).

Rāvaṇa The ten-headed Rākṣasa who abducts Sītā from the hermitage where she, Rāma, and Lakṣmaṇa are living in exile, keeps her in his palace at Laṅkā, and is slain by Rāma in battle. He is the son of Viśravas, who is the half-body transformation of Pulastya (3.258.14), and the female Rākṣasa Puṣpotkaṭā (3.259.7). He performs severe austerities for a thousand years (3.259.14–16) finally cutting off his head and offering it in the fire (3.259.20) out of jealousy of his elder half-brother Kubera, son of Pulastya, who by service to his grandfather Brahmā became immortal, lord of wealth, and ruler of the Rākṣasas with the city Laṅkā as his capital seat. Granted a boon by Brahmā (3.259.22), he chooses invincibility from gods and demons (3.259.25), drives Kubera from Laṅkā (3.259.32), steals his airship Puṣpaka (3.259.34), is consecrated king there (3.259.38), and attacks and robs both demons and gods (3.259.39) because of which, it is said, he is named, 'Rāvaṇa,' which literally means, "he who makes others cry" (3.259.40). In response to the complaints of the gods about him, Brahmā indicates that he has already ordered Viṣṇu to take human form to slay him (3.260.2–5), orders the gods to incarnate also (3.260.6), in particular, to progenerate sons in female bears and monkeys to be Viṣṇu's comrades (3.260.7), and instructs the female Gandharva Dundubhī in how to bring about the desired result as Kaikeyī's hunch-back companion Mantharā (3.260.9–10). He is incited to abduct Sītā to avenge the mutilation of his sister Śūrpaṇakhā's nose and lips (3.261.44–52) by Lakṣmaṇa at Rāma's suggestion (*R.* 3.17.20–21). He coerces his former minister Mārīca to help him abduct Sītā (3.261.55–3.261.10) by drawing Rāma away from the hermitage in the form of a bejeweled deer (3.262.11–13). After Mārīca entices Sītā into sending Rāma to catch him in the form of the bejeweled deer (3.262.17–18) and into goading Lakṣmaṇa after Rāma by crying for help in his voice (3.262.22–29), he approaches Sītā disguised as a Brahman (3.262.16, 3.262.30), reveals himself to her (3.262.32–33), woos her (3.262.34) unsuccessfully (3.262.35–38), runs after her, obstructs her from reentering the hermitage (3.262.39), threatens her unconscious, grabs her by the hair and rises into the sky (3.262.40). He slays the vulture Jaṭāyus who attempts to save her (3.263.2–6) and takes her to his capital city Laṅkā through the sky (3.258.2) where he settles her near an Aśoka grove in his palace (3.264.41) and assigns female Rākṣasas to guard her (3.264.43). He is unable to approach her against her will because he has been cursed by his nephew Nalakūbara after raping his bride (3.264.58–59) to have his head split into a hundred pieces (3.275.33), seven pieces according to the Rāmāyaṇa (*R.* 7.26.23–24, 42–44), if he ever approaches a woman against her will again. He asks her to be his chief queen (3.265.1–16) but is refused (3.265.17–21). He prepares the city for war (3.268.2–6). He gives audience to Rāma's envoy Aṅgada (3.268.7) but infuriated by the message he delivered (3.268.17) signals four Rākṣasas to seize him (3.268.18). After the slaughter of the Rākṣasas who undertake a nocturnal raid on Rāma's camp, Rāvaṇa marches out with his army in the formation of Uśanas (3.269.5) and does battle with Rāma (3.269.7, 11). Informed of the routing of his army and the death of Prahasta and Dhūmrākṣa (3.270.16–18), he awakes his brother Kumbhakarṇa and sends him out against Rāma guarded by Dūṣaṇa's younger brothers Vajravega and Pramāthin (3.270.19–28) and, after hearing of Kumbhakarṇa's death, sends his own son Indrajit out to battle (3.272.1–7). When he sees Indrajit slain, he prepares to kill Sītā (3.273.25–27) but, calmed by Avindhya (3.273.28–32), he marches out against Rāma himself (3.273.33–274.1). He utilizes special powers (3.274.5, 7), emitting Rākṣasas from his body (3.274.6) and creating likenesses of Rāma and Lakṣmaṇa (3.274.8), is attacked by Rāma in Indra's chariot (3.274.17–18), looses various weapons against him (3.274.19, 21–22), becomes afraid (3.274.20), and finally is consumed in flames by Brahmā's weapon (3.274.24–31).

Rudra The god of tempests and father and ruler of the Rudras and Maruts. In the Veda he is closely connected with Indra and still more with Agni, the god of fire, which, as a destroying agent, rages and crackles like the roaring storm, and also with Kāla or Time, the all-consumer, with whom he is afterwards identified; though generally represented as a destroying deity, whose terrible shafts bring death or disease on men and cattle, he has also the epithet *śiva*, 'benevolent' or 'auspicious,' and is even supposed to possess healing powers from his chasing away vapors and purifying the atmosphere. In the later mythology the word *śiva*, which does not occur as a name in the Veda, is employed, first as a euphemistic epithet and then as a real name for Rudra, who lost his special connection with storms and developed into a form of the disintegrating and reintegrating principle; while a new class of beings, described as eleven [or thirty-three] in number, though still called Rudras, took the place of the original Rudras or Maruts. He is reckoned as regent of the northeast quarter. (MW)

Rohiṇī The ninth Nakṣatra or lunar asterism personified as a daughter of Dakṣa (MW), or of Kaśyapa and Surabhi the seventh daughter of Dakṣa (Purāṇic Enc.) called 'the red one' because of the color of the principal star Aldebaran in the constellation of five stars which is figured by a wheeled vehicle or sometimes by a temple or fish (MW). Considered the mother of cows (Purāṇic Enc.). See *MBhCI.* 1.2, p. 269.

Lakṣmaṇa A partial incarnation of Viṣṇu (*R.* 1.17.9), son of Daśaratha and Sumitrā, elder brother of Śatrughna, and younger half brother of Rāma (3.258.7–8). At the time of Rāma's marriage to Sītā, he marries ūrmilā, Janaka's daughter and Sītā's younger sister (*R.* 1.72.18). He follows Rāma to the forest upon his banishment (3.261.28) and accompanies him on all his adventures throughout his exile. Lakṣmaṇa cuts off Rāvaṇa's sister Śūrpaṇakhā's ears and nose at Rāma's suggestion (*R.* 3.17.20–21) when she attacks Sītā intending to eat her (*R.* 3.17.16–18). Instated by Rāma to protect Sītā when at her urging he sets out to catch the bejeweled deer (3.262.18). Although unconvinced by Mārīca's cry to him and Sītā for help in Rāma's voice (3.262.22–24), he sets out after Rāma when Sītā suspects his motives and rebukes him (3.262.25–29) whereupon he encounters Rāma returning to the hermitage and is rebuked by him for abandoning Sītā (3.263.10–14). He is with Rāma when they discover Jaṭāyus, the vulture slain defending her (3.263.16–17). At first despondent upon being seized by the Rākṣasa Kabandha, encouraged by Rāma, he slays him (3.263.26–35). He reassures Rāma when he becomes dejected over Sītā's abduction (3.264.3–7), accompanies Rāma when he makes a treaty with Sugrīva on Mount Ṛśyamūka (3.264.22) and slays Vālin (3.264.37). After several months awaiting action by Sugrīva to find Sītā (3.264.41), he is sent by Rāma to fetch the monkey king (3.266.4–14) whom he brings (3.266.21). He is with Rāma when he hears of Sītā's whereabouts from Hanūmat (3.266.32). He protects the rear of the army of monkeys (3.267.16) as it proceeds south (3.267.15) to the ocean (3.267.21) and is with Rāma when he implores the ocean to allow them to pass (3.267.32). He becomes Vibhīṣaṇa's friend (3.267.49). He breaks down the southern gate of Laṅkā (3.268.24) and slays numerous Rākṣasas (3.268.39), fights with Indrajit (3.269.7) whom he pierces with arrows (3.269.12), saves Sugrīva when he is about to be devoured by Kumbhakarṇa, and burns the Rākṣasa with Brahmā's weapon (3.271.10–17) then is encountered by and does battle with Dūṣaṇa's younger brothers Vajravega and Pramāthin (3.271.19–23). He does battle with Indrajit (3.272.9–15), is brought down by Rāvaṇa's son Indrajit fighting invisible (3.272.21–26), but is restored to consciousness by Vibhīṣaṇa (3.273.5), healed by Sugrīva (3.273.6), and attains the power to see creatures who have disappeared (3.273.9–14). On the advice of Vibhīṣaṇa (3.273.16), he attacks Indrajit before he has completed his morning rites (3.273.17) and slays him (3.273.21–24). When Rāvaṇa creates imitations of Rāma and Lakṣmaṇa which attack them, he advises Rāma to shoot those imitating himself (3.274.8–11). He delights with Rāma upon their victory (3.275.1) but becomes motionless when Rāma initially rejects Sītā (3.275.16). He returns via Kiṣkindhā to Nandigrāma near Ayodhyā with Rāma and Sītā on the aerial car Puṣpaka (3.275.50, 58), where they rejoice on being reunited with Bharata and Śatrughna (3.275.62). He is commanded by Rāma to abandon Sītā on the other side of the Ganges near Valmīki's hermitage (*R.* 7.44.15–17) and does so despite his distress (*R.* 7.45.21, 7.46.2–3, 6, 10, 7.47.14–15) and disagreement (*R.* 7.46.5, 13, 7.49.7–8). When banished by Rāma (7.96.13), he bathes and meditates on the bank of the Sarayū River, becomes invisible and is borne to heaven by Indra where he is welcomed as the fourth part of Viṣṇu returned (*R.* 7.96.15–18).

Laṅkā The capital city (3.258.16, 3.262.33, 3.264.41, 3.266.54, 3.268.21) of Rāvaṇa, after he drove Vaiśravaṇa out, located in a valley on Mount Trikūṭa (3.266.55) on the island also called Laṅkā, present-day Śrīlaṅkā. The city is surrounded by ramparts (3.268.23) with jeweled pillars and defended by various mechanical armaments

(3.268.28–30). Constructed by Viśvakarman (*R.* 5.2.19) and described in *R.* 5.2.8–24, 5.2.47–55, and 5.3.1–13.

Lalāṭākṣī One of the female Rākṣasas assigned to guard Sītā near an Aśoka grove within Rāvaṇa's palace (3.264.44).

Vajrabāhu A monkey warrior devoured by Kumbhakarṇa in the battle at Laṅkā (3.271.4).

Vajravega A Rākṣasa. One of the younger brothers of Dūṣaṇa, the other being Pramāthin, who accompany Kumbhakarṇa out to battle (3.270.27) and are apprehended by Lakṣmaṇa (3.271.20). He is slain by Hanūmat (3.271.24).

Varuṇa Connected with Ouranos and Uranus of Greece and Rome, he is the ancient supreme Vedic deity, called 'king of the gods' or 'king of both gods and men' or 'king of the universe,' described as fashioning and upholding heaven and earth, as possessing extraordinary power and wisdom called *māyā*, as sending his spies or messengers throughout both worlds, as numbering the very winkings of men's eyes, as hating falsehood, as seizing transgressors with his noose (*pāśa*), as inflicting diseases, especially dropsy, as pardoning sin, and as the guardian of immortality (*R̥gveda*). Though not generally regarded in the Veda as a god of the ocean, yet he is often connected with the waters, especially the waters of the atmosphere or firmament, and in one place is called with Mitra *sindhupati* 'lord of the sea or of rivers.' In the later mythology he is god of the ocean, son of Kardama and later of Puṣkara, and is also variously represented as one of the Devagandharvas, as a Nāga, as a king of the Nāgas, and as an Asura. He is the regent of the western quarter and of the Nakṣatra Śatabhiṣaj. (MW)

Vasiṣṭha The preeminent ancient Vedic sage, one of the seven sages, son of Urvaśī by Mitra and Varuṇa, seer of hymns in the seventh maṇḍala of the R̥gveda, Vedic officiant of the Ikṣvākus including Daśaratha and Rāma. According to Nīlakaṇṭha it is he who is called upon by Daśaratha to consecrate Rāma crown prince (3.261.14–15). He and Vāmadeva accompany Bharata in his unsuccessful attempt to bring Rāma back to Ayodhyā from Citrakūṭa (3.261.36) and consecrate Rāma king upon his return to Ayodhyā after the slaying of Rāvaṇa (3.275.65).

Vāmadeva An ancient sage with the patronymic *gautama*, Seer of most of the fourth maṇḍala of the Ṛgveda (RV 4.1–41, 45–48), one of Daśaratha's ministers. He and Vasiṣṭha accompany Bharata in his unsuccessful attempt to bring Rāma back to Ayodhyā from Citrakūṭa (3.261.36) and consecrate Rāma king upon his return to Ayodhyā after the slaying of Rāvaṇa (3.275.65).

Vāyu God of wind, regent of the Nakṣatra Svāti and northwestern quarter, father of Bhīma and Hanūmat.

Vālin The monkey-king of Kiṣkindhā, elder brother of Sugrīva (3.263.41, *R.* 4.9.1–2), and father of Aṅgada (3.266.27, 3.272.14, 17). He is said to be progenerated by Indra (*R.* 1.16.491*1). He chased Māyāvin who challenged him to fight over a woman into a cave after installing Sugrīva to guard its mouth. When Vālin didn't return after a year and he heard the roar of Māyāvin and saw blood emerging from the cave, Sugrīva inferred that Vālin had been killed, blocked the mouth of the cave, and returned to the city where he was crowned king. Vālin, victorious over Māyāvin was furious when he found the cave-mouth blocked and, after managing to emerge, Sugrīva consecrated as king. He banished Sugrīva from the kingdom, took his wife Rumā, imprisoned his friends, and attempted to assassinate him in spite of his explanations, apologies, and gestures to return the kingdom and serve his brother again as he had previously (*R.* 4.8.16–4.10.23). When Sugrīva challenges him after contracting an agreement with Rāma to help him find Sītā in exchange for his slaying Vālin (3.264.14, 3.266.7), Vālin goes out to meet Sugrīva disregarding the cautions of his wife Tārā and suspecting her of sympathizing with Sugrīva (3.264.16–26). He is struck in the heart by Rāma's arrow while fighting with Sugrīva (3.264.27–39) and rebukes Rāma for it (3.264.38). During his reign he is the protector of the honey-forest Madhuvana (3.266.26).

Videha The country in the northeast of India, modern Tirhut, surrounding the city of Mithilā, where Sītā's father Janaka rules.

Vinatā One of Kaśyapa's wives, daughter of Dakṣa, mother of Suparṇa, Aruṇa, and Garuḍa.

Vibhīṣaṇa Son of Viśravas and Mālinī (3.259.8), younger half-brother of Rāvaṇa, who, in spite of being a Rākṣasa, is handsome, virtuous, and devoted to Vedic performances (3.259.9). He undertakes spiritual practice along with his brothers Rāvaṇa and Kumbhakarṇa when they become jealous of their half-brother Vaiśravaṇa's wealth (3.259.15). After a thousand years eating only a withered leaf, engaged in spiritual practice and muttered recitation (3.259.17–18), he is granted a boon by Brahmā and chooses never to think of injustice even if beset by disaster and to obtain Brahmā's weapon (3.259.30). Because of his devotion to dharma in spite of being a Rākṣasa, Brahmā grants him immortality in addition (3.259.31). He follows Vaiśravaṇa when Rāvaṇa expels him from Laṅkā for which Vaiśravaṇa appoints him to the command over the Yakṣa and Rākṣasa armies (3.259.36–37). After Nala constructs his bridge to Laṅkā, Vibhīṣaṇa, with four ministers, approaches Rāma who consecrates him king, adopts him as his counselor, and befriends him to Lakṣmaṇa (3.267.46–49). He advises Rāma to cross to Laṅkā (3.267.50), captures Rāvaṇa's ministers Śuka and Sāraṇa when they penetrate the monkey army in the gardens outside the city of Laṅkā (3.267.52), leads Lakṣmaṇa's troops in an attack on Laṅkā's southern gate (3.268.24), annuls the invisibility of Rākṣasas attacking the monkey troops resting (3.269.3), battles and slays Rāvaṇa's minister Prahasta (3.269.13–3.270.4), revives Rāma and Lakṣmaṇa (3.273.5) after they are made unconscious by Indrajit, presents the eye-salve brought from Kubera by secret messenger, which permits Rāma and his officers to see invisible Rākṣasas (3.273.8–14), advises Lakṣmaṇa to attack Indrajit before he completes his daily rites (3.273.16), and reassures Rāma of the veracity of Mātali's offer to convey him in battle against Rāvaṇa in Indra's chariot (3.274.15–17). After the victory, Rāma presents him the city of Laṅkā (3.275.5). He leads Sītā out of Laṅkā with the aged minister Avindhya and enjoins Rāma to accept her back (3.275.6–7). He leads Rāma riding in the airship Puṣpaka back across Nala's bridge (3.275.51–52), follows him via Kiṣkindhā (3.275.56) to Ayodhyā where he is given leave to depart after Rāma's consecration as king (3.275.66–67).

Virūpākṣa A Rākṣasa who fights with Sugrīva in the war at Laṅkā (3.269.8).

Viśaṁpa Ancestor of Vaiśaṁpāyana.

Viśalyā One of various specific medicinal herbs, Baliospermum axillare (=montanum, see Meulenbeld pp. 544, 561) (called Dantī by Dash, pp. 37–38, Bamber, p. 86), Gloriosa superba (called Kalikārī by Dash pp. 121–122 and Lāṅgalī by Singh and Chunekar pp. 349–350, Bamber p. 587, Cowen, p. 126). It is used by Sugrīva to free Rāma and Lakṣmaṇa from arrows (3.273.6).

Viśravas The reincarnation of the half-body of Pulastya, the mind-born son of Prajāpati (Brahmā 3.259.35), husband of Go, and father of Vaiśravaṇa (3.258.12), who, when his son abandons him for his grandfather Prajāpati, takes birth with half of his body (3.258.14, 3.259.1), in which form he fathers Rāvaṇa, Vibhīṣaṇa, and their other siblings (3.259.6–8).

Viśvakarman The Prajāpati (*Viṣṇupurāṇa* 1.15.119) born to Prabhāsa, the eighth Vasu, of Bṛhaspati's lovely and wise sister who was accomplished in yoga and detached from the world. He is the maker of a thousand arts, the mechanist of the gods, the fabricator of all ornaments, the best of artists, the constructor of the vehicles of the deities, off whose skill humans subsist. Also called Tvaṣṭṛ (3.267.41), he is the younger brother of Aja Ekapād and Ahirbudhnya, elder brother of Rudra, and father of Viśvarūpa (*Śatapathabrāhmaṇa* 1.6.3.1). (*Viṣṇupurāṇa* 1.15.118-121.) The terms *tvaṣṭṛ* and *viśvakarman* may be epithets of the creator of the universe, Brahman, in older literature and may not designate a separate person. The word *tvaṣṭṛ* probably derives from √*tuṣ* 'be satisfied' (analogous to *draṣṭṛ* from √*dṛś*, etc.) rather than from √*takṣ* 'hew' and originally meant the 'enjoyer' rather than the fashioner or carpenter. The tendency to fabricate personalities as the designees of names continues in Purāṇic Encyclopedia 869b which interprets *Viṣṇupurāṇa* 1.15.121 against the commentaries, as listing four sons of Viśvakarman including Tvaṣṭṛ. Thus making Tvaṣṭṛ the son of Viśvakarman would contradict *MBh.* 3.267.41 in which the two names refer to the same person.

Viśvāvasu The radiant Gandharva who emerges from the slain body of Kabandha (q.v.) and directs them to Sugrīva (3.263.36–43).

Viṣṇu One of the principal Hindu deities regarded as 'the preserver,' identified with the supreme deity who incarnates in a portion of his essence on ten principal occasions, including in the sons of Daśaratha, especially Rāma (3.260.5), to deliver mankind from certain great dangers, often identified with Nārāyaṇa, the personified Puruṣa or primeval living spirit described as moving on the waters, reclining on Śeṣa, the serpent of infinity, while the god Brahmā emerges from a lotus growing from his navel. His wives are Lakṣmī or Śrī and even Sarasvatī; his son is Kāmadeva, god of love, and his paradise is called Vaikuṇṭha; he is usually represented with a peculiar mark on his breast called Śrīvatsa, and as holding a śaṅkha 'conch-shell' called *pañcajanya*, a cakra 'discus' called Sudarśana, a gadā 'club' called Kaumodakī, and a padma 'lotus.' He has also a bow called Śārṅga and a sword called Nandaka. His vāhana 'vehicle' is Garuḍa, he has a jewel on his wrist called Syamantaka, another on his breast called Kaustubha, and the river Ganges is said to issue from his foot. He is worshipped under a thousand names, and is sometimes regarded as the divinity of the lunar mansion called Śravaṇa (3.275.65). In Vedic mythology, he assists Indra in killing Vṛtra and drinks the Soma juice with Indra, is a personification of light and of the Sun, especially in his striding over the heavens, which he is said to do in three paces, explained as denoting the threefold manifestations of light in the form of fire, lightning, and the sun, or as designating the three daily stations of the sun in his rising, culminating, and setting. His wives are Aditi and Sinīvālī. (MW)

Vṛtra Vedic demon of darkness and drought who obstructs the waters in the form of rain from the clouds and streams from the mountains. Indra slays him and releases the waters. (Ṛgveda 1.32, 1.52, 4.17–19, 5.32, 8.85, Śatapathabrāhmaṇa 1.1.3, *MBh.* 5.9–10, *Rāmāyaṇa* 7.75–77.) Vṛtra is the serpent son of Tvaṣṭṛ called Dānava because adopted by the mother-father pair Danu and Danāyu. (*Śatapathabrāhmaṇa* 1.6.3.9.)

Vaiśaṁpāyana student of Vyāsa, narrator of the Mahābhārata to Janamejaya, a teacher of the *Taittirīyasaṁhitā*, descendant of Viśaṁpa.

Vaiśravaṇa The god of wealth, regent of the northern quarter, chief of the Yakṣas, a friend of Rudra, owner of the airship Puṣpaka, represented as having three legs and only eight teeth, son of Pulastya (later called Viśravas) by Go or, according to the *Viṣṇupurāṇa* and *Bhāgavatapurāṇa*, Iḍaviḍā, daughter of Tṛṇabindu. He was originally made lord of the Rākṣasas in Laṅkā. When he is driven out by Rāvaṇa he settles on Mount Gandhamādana. While he is commonly called Kubera, this designation occurs only twice in the *Rāmopākhyāna* which favors instead the patronymic Vaiśravaṇa 'son of Viśravan.' 'Viśravan' synonymous with 'Viśravas,' refers to Pulastya's reincarnation of half of himself (3.258.14).

Śatrughna A partial incarnation of Viṣṇu (*R.* 1.17.9), son of Daśaratha and Sumitrā, twin brother of Lakṣmaṇa, and half brother of Rāma and Bharata (3.258.7–8). He is the devoted companion of Bharata as Lakṣmaṇa is to Rāma. At the time of Rāma's marriage to Sītā, he marries Śrutakīrti, daughter of Kuśadhvaja, Janaka's younger brother (*R.* 1.72.20). He accompanies Bharata when he goes to visit his mother's homeland, Kekaya (*R.* 2.1.3), when he goes after Rāma to bring him back (3.261.35), and when he retires to Nandigrāma (*R.* 2.107.8–9) to rule until Rāma's return (3.275.62–63). Consecrated by Rāma as king of the land of Madhu (7.55.7), he slays the Rākṣasa Lavana (*R.* 7.61.34–36) ruling there, and occupies and rules his city (*R.* 7.62.5, 8–9). On the way there he passes a night in Vālmīki's hermitage, during which Sītā gives birth to Kuśa and Lava (*R.* 7.58.10–11). After installing his sons Subāhu and Śatrughātin in Madhurā and Vaidiśa (*R.* 7.98.9), he, along with Bharata, accompanies Rāma in his renunciation (*R.* 7.99.11).

Śanaiścara The planet Saturn, son of the Sun. *MBhCI.* 1.2, p. 270–271.

Śarabhaṅga A seer whose hermitage Rāma, Lakṣmaṇa, and Sītā visit on their way into Daṇḍaka's forest after leaving Citrakūṭa (3.261.39–40).

Śirīṣa A shallow-rooted tree which has pinnate leaves with small, long leaflets dropping in the hot season and which bears innumerable heads of fuzzy, green and white scented flowers in April. (Cowen, p. 38.)

Śiva The deity who contracts the universe at the end of each cycle of ages. Originally a storm deity called Rudra (Ṛgveda) his euphemistic epithet *śiva* 'auspicious one' completely replaced it as his role expanded. He is identified with time in his role as destroyer of the universe but is also given the role of reproduction in which he is worshipped in the form of a phallus. He is identified with the supreme being and regarded as the lord of yoga because of which he is depicted as a renunciate residing in the Himālayas and having matted locks and a third eye of knowledge in the middle of his forehead. After reducing the god of love to ashes for attempting to make him fall in love with her while she served him, he eventually marries Pārvatī, the daughter of Himavat, after being impressed by her renunciation. Regent of the northeastern quarter.

Śuka One of Rāvaṇa's ministers, companion of Sāraṇa, who infiltrates the army of monkeys, is captured by Vibhīṣaṇa, revealed to the monkeys and released by Rāma.

Śūrpaṇakhā Rāvaṇa's younger half-sister, daughter of Viśravas and Rākā, who with her twin brother Khara (3.259.8), serves her elder brothers Rāvaṇa, Kumbhakarṇa and Vibhīṣaṇa when they perform spiritual practice (3.259.19). Desirous to have Rāma or Lakṣmaṇa as her husband, she attacks Sītā intending to eat her (*R.* 3.17.16–18). At Rāma's suggestion Lakṣmaṇa cuts off her ears and nose (*R.* 3.17.20–21). After instigating the conflict between her brother Khara and Rāma (3.261.41), which results in her brother's death (3.261.43), she resorts to Rāvaṇa (3.261.44–45) and reports the matter to him (3.261.51) prompting him to abduct Sītā (3.261.52).

Saṁpāti The vulture king, eldest son of Aruṇa and brother of Jaṭāyus (3.263.1, 3.266.48) who flew too close to the sun in competition with his brother, shielded his brother when he began to faint, scorched his wings and fell to the mountain. He approaches the monkeys sent south in search of Sītā intending to eat them but, after he overhears Aṅgada speak of his brother, he informs them of the location of Rāvaṇa's city Laṅkā and of Sītā's presence there (3.266.46–55, *R.* 4.55.1–4.57.34).

Sahya One of the seven principal mountain ranges in India, where the Godāvarī river has its source in the northwestern Deccan. The monkeys searching the south for Sītā see it near the Malaya range beside the sea (3.266.42).

Sāraṇa One of Rāvaṇa's ministers, companion of Śuka, who infiltrate the army of monkeys, is captured by Vibhīṣaṇa, revealed to the monkeys and released by Rāma.

Sindhu The Indus river or the country of Sindh, through which it flows, ruled over by king Jayadratha who abducts Kṛṣṇā (3.276.10). *MBhCI.* 1.4, p. 478–479.

Sītā Identified with Lakṣmī (*R.* 6.105.25), wife of Rāma, daughter of Janaka, whence her patronymic Jānakī, princess of Videha and of its capital Mithilā whence called Vaidehī and Maithilī. She was created by Brahmā himself (3.258.9), found by Janaka while ploughing and adopted, whence her name *sītā* 'furrow' (*R.* 1.65.14–15, *R.* 2.110.27–30). Janaka promises her to Rāma (*R.* 1.65.27, *R.* 1.66.22–23, *R.* 2.110.48–50) when he lifts, strings, stretches, and breaks Śiva's bow (*R.* 1.66.16–17, *R.* 2.110.46–47). She follows Rāma to the forest when he is banished (3.261.28). Enticed by Rāvaṇa's former minister Mārīca in the form of a bejeweled deer, she sends Rāma after it (3.262.11–12, 17). When she hears Mārīca imitating the voice of Rāma call to her and Lakṣmaṇa, she runs towards it and, when Lakṣmaṇa reassures her, rebukes him out of suspicion of his motives (3.262.22–28). Left alone after Lakṣmaṇa sets out to find Rāma (3.262.29), she offers fruit and roots to Rāvaṇa (3.262.31) when he arrives disguised as a Brahman (3.262.30). She refuses his invitations to become his queen (3.262.34) and turns to reenter her dwelling (262.35–29) but she faints when threatened by him, is seized by the hair, and is abducted through the sky (3.262.40). She cries out for Rāma (3.262.41), is unsuccessfully attempted to be rescued by the vulture Jaṭāyus (3.263.2–6), drops her jewelry near hermitages, lakes, and rivers (3.263.7), and a bright yellow garment amidst Sugrīva and his ministers on Mount Ṛśyamūka (3.263.8–9, 3.264.12). She lives on fruit and roots, fasting and meditating, wearing the simple dress of spiritual practitioners, smeared with dirt, near an Aśoka grove within Rāvaṇa's palace, guarded by female Rākṣasas (3.264.41–44, 3.266.58). Although threatened constantly she refuses to consent to Rāvaṇa's proposals and remains devoted to her husband (3.264.45–51). She is consoled by the female Rākṣasa Trijaṭā with a message from the aged Rākṣasa Avindhya (3.264.53–72). Wooed by Rāvaṇa (3.265.8–16), she rejects his proposals (3.265.17–24). When Hanūmat visits her by the Aśoka grove (3.266.59–63) she gives him an ornament to take back to Rāma and tells him the story of Rāma destroying a crow who assaulted her (3.266.64–67). After Rāvaṇa's defeat, she is lead out of the city by Vibhīṣaṇa and presented to Rāma by the aged Rākṣasa Avindhya (3.275.6–7). Initially rejected by Rāma (3.275.10–13), she faints (3.275.14–15). After everyone becomes motionless (3.275.16) and the gods appear (3.275.17–20), she stands up and asks the god of wind (Mātariśvan) and the five elements to take her life if she has sinned (3.275.21–24). After Vāyu,

Agni, Varuṇa, Brahmā, and Daśaratha request him to take her back (3.275.25–35), Rāma reunites with her (3.275.38). In the Rāmāyaṇa, she is restored to Rāma by Agni (*R.* 6.106.3–9) and accepted (*R.* 6.106.10–20). She grants fame equal to Rāma's and divine enjoyments to Hanūmat (3.275.43–44). She returns with Rāma on the aerial car Puṣpaka (3.275.52) via Kiṣkindhā (3.275.56) to Ayodhyā (3.275.50). She becomes pregnant (*R.* 7.41.21–22) and Rāma grants (*R.* 7.41.26) her wish to visit the hermitages by the Ganges the next day (*R.* 7.41.23–25). Because of complaints about the example he set by accepting her back (*R.* 7.42.16–19), out of his concern for public opinion (*R.* 7.87.14–15, 20, *R.* 7.88.3), at Rāma's command (*R.* 7.44.15–17) she is taken to the other side of the Ganges near Valmīki's hermitage and abandoned by Lakṣmaṇa (7.46.13–15, 7.47.14–15). She gives birth to twin sons Kuśa and Lava in Vālmīki's hermitage (*R.* 7.58.1–2, 5–6). After Rāma recognizes his sons when they have completed their recitation of the *Rāmāyaṇa* (*R.* 7.86.2), at Rāma's request (*R.* 7.86.4–6) she is led before him by Vālmīki (*R.* 7.87.9, 13) and presented to him with his sons (*R.* 7.87.14–16) for the purpose of proving her fidelity (*R.*7.87.20). She asks the earth to give her a space if she has never thought of anyone other than Rāma (*R.* 7.88.9–10). The goddess Earth rises up out of the earth on a throne, takes her in her arms, seats her on the throne, and disappears again into the earth amidst a rain of flowers and praises of the gods and all gathered there (7.88.11–20).

Sugrīva The monkey-king, younger brother of Vālin (3.263.41, *R.* 4.9.1–2), son of the Sun (*R.* 1.16.19, 491*2), who helps Rāma find and recover Sītā with his army (3.258.3) after Rāma helps him slay his elder brother, become king of Kiṣkindhā, and recover his wife Rumā (*R.* 4.20.19, *R.* 4.25.38). Vālin had banished him from the kingdom and taken his wife Rumā (*R.* 4.8.16–4.10.23, *R.* 4.18.19). He is dwelling on Mount Ṛśyamūka near the river Pampā with four ministers, Mainda, Dvivida, Hanūmat, son of the wind, and Jāmbavat, king of the bears (3.264.23), when Rāma and Lakṣmaṇa come to him (3.264.9–11) after being sent to him by the Gandharva Viśvāvasu who emerged from the slain body of Kabandha (3.263.38–41). He sends Hanūmat to greet them (3.264.10), shows Rāma the garment Sītā dropped while being abducted by Rāvaṇa (3.264.12, 3.263.8–

9), and contracts an agreement to recover Sītā in exchange for Rāma's slaying Vālin (3.264.14–15, 21). He goes to Kiṣkindhā accompanied by Rāma, Lakṣmaṇa and his ministers and challenges Vālin (3.264.15–16). After accusing him of taking his wife and kingdom (3.264.29) he falls to fighting Vālin (3.264.30–32). Hanūmat puts a garland around his neck so that Rāma can distinguish him from Vālin whom he pierces in the heart with an arrow (3.264.33–36). Sugrīva returns to Kiṣkindhā and to his former wife Tārā (3.264.39) and attends to Rāma on Mount Mālyavat (3.264.40, 3.266.1, 61) while he dispatches monkeys in all directions to search for Sītā. Suspected by Rāma of failing to fulfill his side of their agreement (3.266.5–10) and so informed by Lakṣmaṇa (3.266.14), he defends himself and informs Lakṣmaṇa that he instructed the monkeys he sent to search for Sītā to return in a month, five days thence (3.266.15–20), and accompanies Lakṣmaṇa to see Rāma (3.266.21). Informed after two months that the monkeys who searched the south have returned and are devouring the honey-forest Madhuvana (3.266.25–27), he infers that they have found Sītā (3.266.28) and reports it to Rāma (3.266.29). His inference is subsequently verified in Hanūmat's report (3.266.30–68). He musters a large army (3.267.1–13) and marches forth with Rāma (3.267.15). He suspected Vibhīṣaṇa of being a spy when he approaches Rāma after Nala constructs his bridge to Laṅkā (3.267.47). He fights with Virūpākṣa during Rāvaṇa's first battle with Rāma (3.269.8), and with Kumbhakarṇa by whom he is nearly eaten before being saved by Lakṣmaṇa (3.271.6–13). He surrounds Rāma and Lakṣmaṇa with monkey-leaders when they are struck down by Indrajit (3.273.3) and heals their wounds with the medicinal herb Viśalyā and sacred formulas (3.273.6). He is one of those who gain the ability to see the invisible by applying Kubera's water (3.273.13). He accompanies Rāma via Kiṣkindhā (3.275.50, 55), where he and Rāma give Sītā a tour of the forest in the airship Puṣpaka (3.275.56), to Ayodhyā where he is given leave to depart after Rāma's consecration as king (3.275.66–67).

Sumitrā One of the wives of Daśaratha, mother of Lakṣmaṇa and Śatrughna (3.258.8).

Suṣeṇa One of Sugrīva's monkey-generals (3.267.2), son of Varuṇa (3.267.2, *R.* 1.16.491*11) or Dhanvantari, father of Tārā, physician of Sugrīva. He is among those who surround Rāma and Lakṣmaṇa when Indrajit binds them with lattices of arrows (3.273.4).

Hanūmat Son of the wind (3.266.26, *R.* 1.16.491*13–15) and Añjanā, minister of the monkey king Sugrīva. He is one of the four companions living with Sugrīva on Mount Ṛśyamūka when Sītā drops a garment in their midst while she is being abducted by Rāvaṇa (3.263.8–9) and when Rāma and Lakṣmaṇa are first sent to Sugrīva (3.263.38–41). Hanūmat greets them and brings them to Sugrīva (3.264.10–11). He accompanies Sugrīva when he goes to Kiṣkindhā to challenge Vālin (3.264.23) and puts a garland around his neck during their fight so that Rāma can distinguish him from his brother Vālin (3.264.33–35). He heads the monkeys dispatched by Sugrīva to search for Sītā in the southern direction (*R.* 4.44.5) who reveal their success by devouring the protected honey-forest Madhuvana upon their return (3.266.26–28) before approaching Sugrīva in the presence of Rāma and Lakṣmaṇa with their news (3.266.30–32). He reports his success in detail to Rāma (3.266.36–68) including how he leapt across the straits to Laṅkā (3.266.57), saw and conversed with Sītā (3.266.58–67) who present him a jewel and told him the story of Rāma slaying the crow who molested her at Citrakūṭa to serve as proof that he had found her (3.266.66–67), and burned the city before returning (3.266.68). He is the vanguard of Sugrīva's army when it sets out for Laṅkā (3.267.16), stands his ground and regroups the monkeys when Dhūmrākṣa sets them to flight (3.270.7–8), fights and slays Dhūmrākṣa with his huge body (3.270.11–14), is among those who surround Rāma and Lakṣmaṇa when they are struck down by Indrajit (3.273.4), those who gain the ability to see the invisible Rākṣasas by applying the water sent by Vaiśravaṇa (3.273.13), and those who surround Rāvaṇa when he comes out to fight (3.274.3). He is granted boons by Sītā after her reunion with Rāma (3.275.43–44) and is dispatched by Rāma as herald to Bharata when they return to Ayodhyā (3.275.59–60).

Hari One of the Piśāca and Rākṣasa warriors who attack Rāma's troops invisible while they are resting, are exposed by Vibhīṣaṇa, and slain (3.269.1–4).

Himavat The Himalayan range. *MBhCI.* 1.4, p. 486–499.

Genealogy

Table 1
Rāma's genealogy (258.6–10)

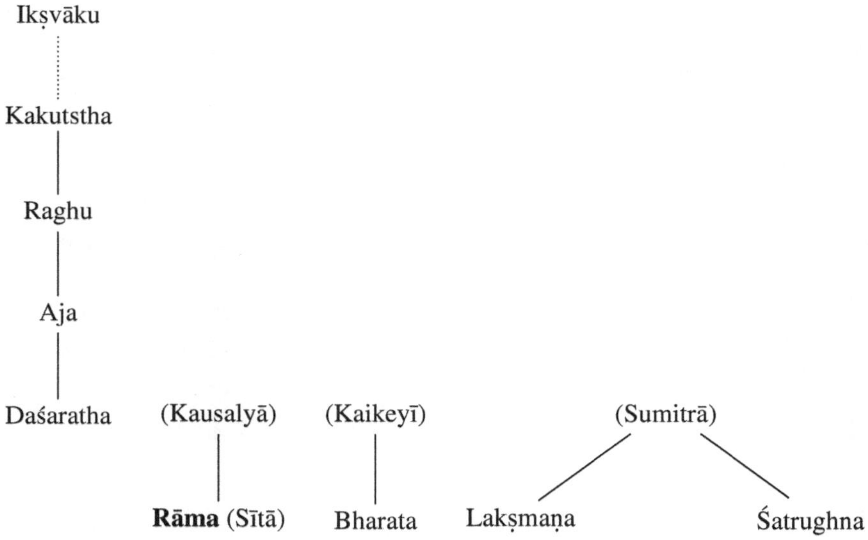

Table 2

Rāvaṇa's genealogy (258.11–259.9)

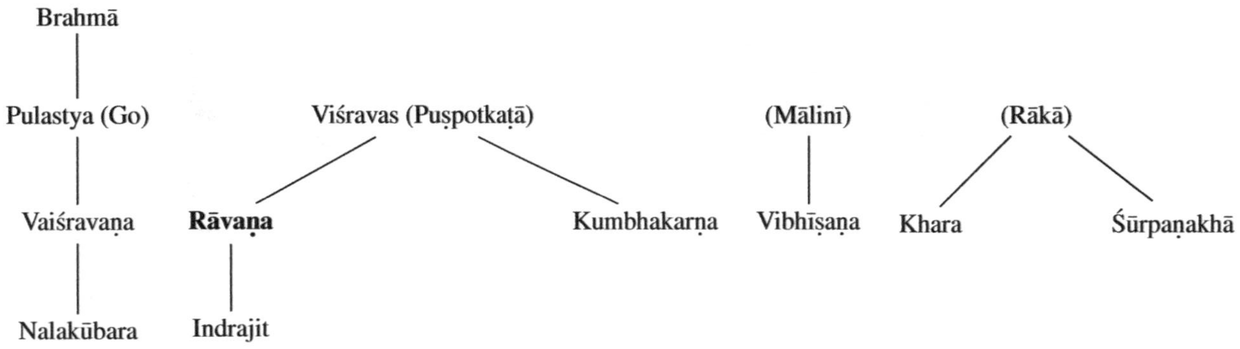

Bibliography

1. Related books by the author

2. Critical editions of the epics

Bhatt, G. H., U. P. Shah, et al., eds. *The Vālmīki-Rāmāyaṇa: critically edited for the first time*. 7 vols. Vol. I, *The Bālakāṇḍa*, ed. G. H. Bhatt, 1960; Vol. II, *The Ayodhyākāṇḍa*, ed. P. L. Vaidya, 1962; Vol. 3, *The Araṇyakāṇḍa*, ed. P. C. Divanji, 1963; Vol. 4, *The Kiṣkindhākāṇḍa*, ed. D. R. Mankad, 1965; Vol. 5, *The Sundarakāṇḍa*, ed. G. C. Jhala, 1966; Vol. 6, *The Yuddhakāṇḍa*, ed. P. L. Vaidya, 1971; Vol. 7, *The Uttarakāṇḍa*, ed. U. P. Shah, fasc. 1, 1972, fasc. 2, 1973, fasc. 3, 1975. Baroda: Oriental Institute, 1960–1975.

Kinjawadekar, Ramchandrashastri, ed. *The Mahābhāratam with the Bharata Bhawadeepa commentary of Nīlkaṇṭha: Srīḥ Mahābhāratam caturdharavaṁśāvataṁsaśrīmannīlakaṇṭhaviracitabhāratabhāva-dīpākhyaṭīkayā sametam*. 6 vols. Vols. 2, 3 *Vana Parva*. New Delhi: Oriental Books Reprint Corporation, 1979.

Sukthankar, Vishnu Sitaram et al., eds. *The Mahābhārata*. 19 vols. Vol. 4, *The Āraṇyakaparvan (part 2)*, ed. Vishnu S. Sukthankar, 1942. Pune: Bhandarkar Oriental Research Institute, 1933–1959.

3. English translations of the epics

Arya, Ravi Prakash, ed. *Ramayana of Valmiki: Sanskrit text and English translation*. Trans. by M. N. Dutt. Delhi: Parimal Publications, 1998.

Dutt, Manmatha Nath, trans. *A prose English translation of the Mahabharata*. 6 vols. Calcutta: H. C. Dass, Elysium Press, 1895–1905. [Reprint: 7 vols. Delhi: Parimal Publications, 1994.]

Egenes, Linda and Kumuda Reddy. *The Ramayana: a new retelling of Valmiki's ancient epic–complete and comprehensive*. Tarcher cornerstone editions. New York: A TarcherPerigee Book, 2016.

Goldman, Robert P., ed. *The Ramayana of Valmiki: an epic of ancient India*. Princeton Library of Asian translations. Vol. 1, *Bālakāṇḍa*, tr. Robert P. Goldman, 1984; Vol. 2, *Ayodhyākāṇḍa*, tr. Sheldon I. Pollock, 1986; Vol. 3, *Araṇyakāṇḍa*, tr. Sheldon I. Pollock, 1991; Vol. 4, *Kiṣkindhākāṇḍa*, tr. Rosalind Lefeber, 1994; Vol. 5, *Sundarakāṇḍa*, tr. Robert P. Goldman and Sally J. Sutherland Goldman, 1996; Vol. 6, *Yuddhakāṇḍa*, tr. Robert P. Goldman, Sally J. Sutherland Goldman and Barend A. van Nooten, 2009; Vol. 7, *Uttarakāṇḍa*, tr. Robert P. Goldman and Sally J. Sutherland Goldman, 2016. Princeton, New Jersey: Princeton University Press, 1984–1996.

Goldman, Robert P., Sheldon I. Pollock, Rosalind Lefeber, Sally J. Sutherland Goldman, and Barend A. van Nooten, trans. *Ramayana*. 5. Clay Sanskrit Library. In English and Sanskrit (romanized) on facing pages. Volumes 6–7 forthcoming. New York: New York University Press; JJC Foundation, 2005–2006.

Srimad Valmiki Ramayanam. Trans. by N. Raghunathan. 3 vols. Madras; Bangalore: Vighneswara Publishing House, 1981.

The Mahābhārata. Trans. by Johannes Adrianus Bernardus van Buitenen. 3 vols. Chicago: Chicago University Press, 1973–1978.

The Mahabharata of Krishna-Dwaipayana Vyasa. Trans. by Kisari Mohan Ganguli. 5th ed. 12 vols. Calcutta: Pratap Chandra Roy and Sundari Bala Roy, 1883–1896. [Reprint: New Delhi: Munshiram Manoharlal, 1990-91.]

4. Production in audiovisual media

Lutgendorf, Philip. "All in the (Raghu) Family: a video epic in cultural context." In: *The life of Hinduism*. Ed. by John Stratton Hawley and Vasudha Narayanan. The Life of Religion. Berkeley: University of California Press, 2006, pp. 140–57.

—. "Ramayan: the video." In: *The drama review* 34.2 (1990), 127–76.

—. *The life of a text: performing the Ramcharitmanas of Tulsidas*. Berkeley: University of California Press, 1991.

Nizokami, Tomio, ed. *Rāmāyaṇa: TV serial script*. Produced and directed by Ramanand Sagar, transcribed by Girish Bakshi. 2 vols. Osaka: Osaka University of Foreign Studies, 1992.

Sagar, Anand, director and producer. *Rāmāyaṇa*. The television serial originally broadcast on NDTV Imagine; music by Ravindra Jain. Mumbai: Sagar Art Enterprises, 2008.

Sagar, Ramanand, director and producer. *Rāmāyaṇa*. 17 videodiscs. Condensed from the television serial originally broadcast in 78 episodes in 1987-1988; research & adaptation by Phani Majumdar; music by Ravindra Jain. Mumbai: Sagar Art Enterprises, 2001. [Republished: Gayatri Films & Music, 2006.]

Singh, Mukesh, Pawan Parkhi, and Rajesh Shikhre, directors. *Rāmāyaṇa: jīvan kā ādhār*. Produced by Meenakshi Sagar and Moti Sagar. Television serial originally broadcast on Zee TV. Mumbai: Sagar Art Enterprises, Aug. 12, 2012–Sept. 1, 2013.

Sternfeld, Michael, dramatic reader. *Ram's dharma: leadership secrets from the ultimate warrior-sage-prince*. 1: *Bala & Ayodhya kandas*. Vedic Audio Knowledge, 2014.

Sternfeld, Michael and Krishna Das, dramatic readers. *Hanuman's leap of faith: harnessing the power of love and devotion in our lives*. Vedic Audio Knowledge, 2022.

Sternfeld, Michael, Richard Ross, and Stephen White, dramatic readers. *The Ramayana of Valmiki: a dramatic audio production in English of the unabridged Srimad Valmiki Ramayanam translated from the Sanskrit by N. Raghunathan*. 3. Fairfield, Iowa: Vedic Audio Knowledge, 1998–2004.

5. Research on the story of Rāma

Agrawal, Bhanu. *Valmiki ramayana in Malwa painting*. Varanasi: Ganga Kaveri Publication House, 1995.

Agrawal, Jagannath. "The authenticity of the Uttarakanda of Valmiki's Ramayana." In: *Vishveshvaranand Indological Journal* 13.2 (1975), 1–5.

Armelin, Indumati. "Les cent huit Ramayana de Moropant (1729-1794)." In: *Journal Asiatique* 276.3–4 (1988), 335–47.

Bailey, Greg and Mary Brockington, eds. *Epic threads: John Brockington on the Sanskrit epics*. Oxford; New Delhi; New York: Oxford University Press, 2000.

Baumgartner, Alexander. *Rāmāyaṇa und die Rāma-Literatur der Inder*. Salzwasser-Verlag GMBH, 2016.

Berg, Jessica. *Rāmāyaṇa and Mahābhārata in stone: the narrative friezes of the Kr̥ṣṇa temple at Pāṭan, Nepal*. Ph.D. dissertation, Humboldt-Universität zu Berlin, 2020. Baden-Baden: Ergon Verlag, 2022.

Blackburn, Stuart H. "Hanging in the balance: Rama in the shadow puppet theater of Kerala." In: *Papers from South Asia Seminar at the Univ. of Pennsylvania, 1987–88: gender, genre, and power in South Asian expressive traditions*. Ed. by Arjun Appadurai, Frank J. Korom, and Margaret A. Mills. South Asia Seminar Series. Philadelphia: University of Pennsylvania, 1991, pp. 379–94.

—. *Inside the drama-house*. Berkeley, California: University of California Press, 1996.

—. *Rama stories and shadow puppets: Kampa-n's Ramayana in performance*. Delhi: Oxford University Press, 1997.

Bose, Mandakranta, ed. *A varied optic: contemporary studies in the Rāmāyaṇa*. Papers from the conference, The Rāmāyaṇa Culture: Text, Performance, Iconography, and Gender, held in Vancouver, Feb. 20-21, 1999. Vancouver: Institute of Asian Research, The University of British Columbia, 2000.

—. ed. *The Rāmāyaṇa culture: text, performance, and iconography*. New Delhi: D. K. Printworld, 2003. [Revised second edition of Bose 2000.]

—. *The Rāmāyaṇa in Bengali folk paintings*. New Delhi: Niyogi Books, 2017.

—. ed. *The Rāmāyaṇa revisited*. Oxford: Oxford University Press, 2004.

Bose, Priyadarshini. *Woman's Rāmāyaṇa: Candravatī's Bengali epic*. Abingdon; New York: Routledge, 2017.

Botto, Oscar, ed. *Indologica taurinensia*. 19–20 (1993/1994): *Proceedings of the Ninth International Ramayana Conference (Torino, April 13th-17th, 1992)*. Torino, Italy: Edizioni A.I.T., 1995.

Brockington, John Leonard. *Righteous Rāma: the evolution of an epic.* Delhi: Oxford University Press, 1985.

—. "Sanskrit epic tradition: I. Epic and epitome (Rāmāyaṇa and Rāmopākhyāna)." In: *Indological Taurinensia* 6 (1978). Proceedings of the Third World Sanskrit Conference, Paris, 20-25 June 1977, 79–111.

—. *The Sanskrit epics.* Handbuch der Orientalistik. 2. Abt., Indien 12. Leiden: Brill, 1998.

—. "The textualization of the Sanskrit epics." In: *Trends in linguistics, studies and monographs* 128 (2000), 193–216.

—. "Translating the Sanskrit epics." In: *Indological Taurinensia* 28 (2002), 97–126.

Brockington, John Leonard, Mary Brockington, and Mandakranta Bose, eds. *The other Rāmāyaṇa women: regional rejection and response.* Routledge Hindu Studies Series. London and New York: Routledge, 2016.

Brockington, John Leonard and Danuta Stasik. *Indian epic traditions — past and present.* Rocznik Orientalistyczny 54. Warszawa: Wydawnictwo Naukowe, 2002.

Brockington, Mary, ed. *Stages and transitions: temporal and historical frameworks in epic and Purāṇic literature.* proceedings of the Second Dubrovnik International Conference on the Sanskrit Epics and Purāṇas, August 1999. Zagrab: Croatian Academy of Sciences and Arts, 2002.

Brockington, Mary and Peter Schreiner, eds. *Composing a tradition: concepts, techniques and relationships.* Zagrab: Croatian Academy of Sciences and Arts, 1999.

Chambard, Jean Luc. "Le Ramayana des femmes dans un village de l'Inde centrale." In: *Cahiers de litterature orale* 32 (1992), 101–24.

Chandra, Lokesh. "The Rama epic in South East Asia." In: *Indian Horizons* 23.1 (1974), 32–35.

Clines, Gregory M. *Jain Rāmāyaṇa narratives: moral vision and literary innovation.* Routledge advances in Jaina studies. London; New York: Routledge, 2022.

Craven, Roy C., ed. *Ramayana: pahari paintings.* Bombay: Marg Publications, 1990.

Daalen, L. A. van. "Two notes on Ramayana textual criticism." In: *Brahmavidyā: The Adyar Library Bulletin* 50 (1986), 402–17.

Desai, Santosh N. "Ramayana: an instrumental of historical contact and cultural transmission between India and Asia." In: *Journal of Asian Studies* 30.1 (1970), 5–20.

Dev Sen, Nabaneeta. "A woman's retelling of the Rama-tale: Chandrabati Ramayana re-read in 1990." In: *New Visions of Creation: feminist innovations in literary theory*. Proceedings of the XIIIth Congress of International Comparative Literature Association, Tokyo, 1991. Ed. by Maria Elena de Valdes and Margaret R. Higonnet. Force of Vision 5. Tokyo: University of Tokyo Press, 1993, pp. 95–104.

Dhar, Aarttee Kaul. *Sita in the Ramayana traditions*. New Delhi: Adhyayan Publishers & Distributors, 2016.

Dwivedi, Lava Kush Prasad. "Role of the concurrent cultures in the cultural make-up of the Ramayana age." In: *Journal of the Oriental Institute, Baroda* 36.1–4 (Sept. 1986–June 1987), 61–67.

Embree, Ainslie T. *The Ramayana in modern India: Hinduizing India's national discourse*. East-West Center working papers, Education and training series 2. Honolulu, Hawaii: East-West Center, 1995.

Evans, Kirsti. *Epic narratives in the Hoysala temples: the Ramayana, Mahabharata, and Bhagavata Purana in Halebid, Belur, and Amrtapura*. Studies in the history of religions 74. Leiden; New York: Brill, 1997.

Goldman, Robert P. *A clouded mirror: the Uttarakāṇḍa of the Vālmīkirāmāyaṇa as an occluded guide to statecraft*. DVD video: NTSC color broadcast system. Seattle, Washington, 2016.

—. *The Vālmīki Rāmāyaṇa as epic and Dharmaśāstra: reading the Ādikāvya as an ethical guide*. Three lectures delivered at the Department of Philosophy at Jadavpur University in December 2016. Kolkata: Department of Philosophy, Jadavpur University and D. K. Printworld, 2021.

Goswami, Mamani Rayachama. *Ramayana from Ganga to Brahmaputra*. New Delhi: B. R. Publishing, 1996.

Haditjaroko, Sunardjo. *Living shadows: Ramayana*. New York: Vantage Press, 1963.

—. *Ramayana: our national reader*. Jakarta: Djambatan, 1961.

—. *Ramayana: Indonesian wayang show*. Jakarta: Djambatan, 1981.

Herman, Phyllis Kaplan. "Ideal kingship and the feminine power: a study of the depiction of Ramarajya in the Valmiki Ramayana." Ph.D. diss. Los Angeles: University of California, Los Angeles, 1979.

Hess, Linda. "Rejecting Sita: Indian responses to the ideal man's cruel treatment of his ideal wife." In: *Journal of the American Academy of Religion* 67.1 (Mar. 1999), 1–32.

Hiltebeitel, Alf. "Religious studies and Indian epic texts." In: *Religious Studies Review* 21 (Jan. 1995), 26–32.

Hossick, Malcolm, ed. *Rama and Sita: the study and performance of Thai dance*. eVideo. New York: Films Media Group, 2012.

Indonesian Ramayana: the Uttarakanda. Trans. by I. Gusti Putu Phalgunadi. New Delhi: Sundeep Prakashan, 1999.

Iyengar, K. Srinivasa, ed. *Asian variations in Ramayana*. Papers presented at the international seminar on "Variations in Ramayana in Asia: Their Cultural, Social, and Anthropological Significance," New Delhi, January 1981. New Delhi: Sahitya Akademi, 1983.

Jain, Rajendra. *Ramayana theatre in India*. Delhi: R. R. Pubishing Corporation, 1996.

Jamindar, Rasesh. "The Rama story and Mallavadisuri." In: *Journal of the Oriental Institute, Baroda* 17 (1968), 237–39.

Joshi, Devdatta. "The Akhyana of Lava and Kusa in the Medieval Gujarati Literature in the Light of the Valmiki Ramayana." In: *Journal of the Oriental Institute, Baroda* 39.1–2 (Sept.–Dec. 1989), 35–43.

Kam, Garrett. *Ramayana in the arts of Asia*. Select Books, 2000.

Kapp, Dieter B. "The 'Alu Kurumba Ramayana': the story of Rama as narrated by a South Indian tribe." In: *Asian Folklore Studies* 48.1 (1989), 123–40.

Keislar, Allan Mott. "Search for the Bhusundi-ramayana: one text or many?: the Adi-ramayana, the Bhusundi-ramayana, and the Ramayana-maha-malma." Ph.D. diss. University of California, Berkeley, Dec. 1998.

Kern, H., ed. *Rāmāyaṇa: The Story of Rāma and Sītā in Old Javanese*. Romanized edition by Willem van der Molen. Javanese Studies: Contributions to the Study of Javanese Literature, Culture and History 1. Tokyo: Research Institute for Languages, Cultures of Asia, and Africa, Tokyo University of Foreign Studies, 2015.

Khing, Hoc Dy. *Un épisode du Ramayana khmer: Rama endormi par les maléfices de Vaiy Rabn.* Recherches asiatiques. Paris: l'Harmattan, 1995.

Krishnamoorthy, K., ed. *Critical inventory of Ramayana studies in the world: Indian languages and English.* Vol. 1. 1992.

Krishnan, Gauri Parimoo. *Ramayana: a living tradition.* National Heritage Board, 1997.

Kumar, Anthony Amit. "Forgotten Sītā: the significance of the mother goddess in the Rāmāyaṇa." M.A. diss. University of the West, 2016.

Le Sauce-Carnis, Marion. "Du héros épique à l'icône divine: L'image de Rāma dans les décors sculptés de l'empire de Vijayanagar." Ph.D. diss. Sorbonne Paris Cité, 2016.

Losty, Jeremiah P. *15 paintings depicting the adventures of Hanumān on Laṅkā from the Rāmāyaṇa.* London: Simon Ray (Gallery), 2016.

Majumdar, R. C. "Ramayana Outside India." In: *Indo Asian Culture* 19.2 (1970), 42–45.

Manavalan, A. A. *Ramayana: a comparative study of Ramakathas.* Trans. by C. T. Indra and Prema Jagannathan. Translated from the Tamil *Irāma kātaïyum Irāmāyaṇaṅkaḷum.* Bryn Mawr, Pennsylvania: Global Collective Publishers, 2022.

Matilal, Bimal Krishna. "Rāma's Moral Decisions." In: *Dr. K. Kunjunni Raja Felicitation Volume.* Ed. by Radha Burnier et al., pp. 344–51.

McGill, Forrest, Pika Ghosh, Robert P. Goldman, Sally J. Sutherland Goldman, and Philip Lutgendorf. *The Rama epic: hero, heroine, ally, foe.* San Francisco: Asian Art Museum, 2016.

Mishra, Rajendra. "Rāmāyaṇa tradition after Vālmīki in India and abroad." In: *Indological Taurinensia* 36 (2010), 67–76.

—. *Suvarnadvipiya Ramakatha: Ramayana episode in Indonesia.* Rajata jayanti granthamala 22. New Delhi: Rashtriya Samskrta Samsthana, 1996.

Moertjipto et al. *The Ramayana reliefs of Prambanan.* Yogyakarta: Penerbit Kanisius, 1991.

Mohamad, Zulkifli. "Seri Rama-Siti Dewi: Ramayana epic in Malaysian contemporary dance theatre." In: *Green Mill Dance Project (4th: 1996: Melbourne, Vic.) World dance '96: new dance from old cultures*, pp. 62–70.

Pandey, Shyam Manohar. "Abduction of Sita in the Ramayana of Tulasidasa." In: *Orientalia Lovaniensia Periodica* 8 (1977), 263–88.

Patani, Rajana. *Ramayana*. Amadavada: Shri Lakshmi Pustaka Bhandara, 1998.

Phutthaphōchān. *The Buddhist Rāmāyaṇa = Phra Lak Phar Lām: original text, translation and critical study*. Ed. and trans. by Sachchidanand Sahai. 2nd ed. Delhi: Buddhist World Press, 2016.

Pollet, Gilbert, ed. *Indian epic values: Ramayana and its impact*. Proceedings of the 8th International Ramayana Conference, Leuven, 6-8 July 1991. Orientalia Lovaniensia analecta 66. Leuven: Uitgeverij Peeters en Dep. Oosterse Studies, 1995.

Pou, Saveros. "Indigenization of Ramayana in Cambodia." In: *Asian Folklore Studies* 51.1 (1992), 89–102.

Raghavan, V. *The Ramayana tradition in Asia: Papers presented at the international seminar on the Ramayana tradition in Asia, New Delhi, December, 1975*. New Delhi; Calcutta; Madras; Bombay: Sahitya Akademi, 1980.

Raju, B. Rama. "Sanskrit works with Ramayana theme written by Andhras." In: *Journal of the Oriental Institute, Baroda* 16 (1966), 149–56.

Ramayana, an Asian cultural confluence: a dance-drama presesentation by the Temple of Fine Arts International. Kuala Lumpur: Hansa Designs, 1996.

Rao, Ajay K. *Re-figuring the Rāmāyaṇa as theology: a history of reception in premodern India*. Routledge Hindu Studies Series 9. London and New York: Routledge, 2015.

Richman, Paula, ed. *Many Rāmāyaṇas: the diversity of a narrative tradition in South Asia*. Berkeley; Los Angeles: University of California Press, 1991.

—. *Ramayana stories in modern South India: an anthology*. Bloomington: Indiana University Press, 2008.

Richman, Paula and Rustom Bharucha, eds. *Performing the Ramayana traditions: enactments, interpretations, and arguments*. New York: Oxford University Press, 2021.

Robson, Stuart, trans. *The Old Javanese Rāmāyaṇa: a new English translation with an introduction and notes*. Javanese Studies: Contributions to the Study of Javanese Literature, Culture and History 2. Tokyo: Research Institute for Languages, Cultures of Asia, and Africa, Tokyo University of Foreign Studies, 2015.

Rooney, Dawn. *The Thiri Rāma: finding Rāmāyaṇa in Myanmar*. Abingdon, Oxon; New York, NY: Routledge, 2017.

Sahai, Sachchidanand. "Sources of the Lao Ramayana tradition." In: *Indian Horizons* 21.2–3 (1972), 70–81.

—. "The Khvay Thuaraphi: an unpublished Laotian version of the Ramayana." In: *Vishveshvaranand Indological Journal* 15 (1977), 33–51.

Sardar, Marika. *Epic tales from ancient India: paintings from the San Diego Museum of Art*. San Diego: San Diego Museum of Art, 2017.

Scharf, Peter M. "Public and private ethics concerning a woman's fidelity in various versions of the story of Rāma." Paper presented to the Department of Classics, Brown University, 24 February 1999. Revised paper presented at the 209th Meeting of the American Oriental Society, 21-24 March 1999, Baltimore. [Forthcoming.]

Sen, Dineshchandra. *The Bengali Ramayanas: being lectures delivered to the Calcutta University in 1916, as Ramtanu Lahiri research fellow in the history of Bengali language and literature*. Calcutta: University of Calcutta, 1920. [Reprint: Delhi: Amar Prakashan, 1987.]

Seyller, John, Marika Sardar, and Audrey Truschke. *The Ramayana of Hamida Banu Begum, Queen Mother of Mughal India*. Complete illustrated Persian manuscript with essays. Doha, Qatar: Museum of Islamic Art; Cinisello Balsamo, Milano: Silvana editoriale, 2020.

Seyller, John William. *Workshop and patron in Mughal India: the Freer Ramayana and other illustrated manuscripts of 'Abd al-Rahim*. Supplementum 42. Zürich, Switzerland; Washington, D.C.: Artibus Asiae Publishers: Museum Rietberg in association with the Freer Gallery of Art, Smithsonian Institution, 1999.

Shanti Bardhan's Ramayana. Great masters series. Videocassette of performance by the Little Ballet Troupe. Delhi: Indira Gandhi National Centre for Arts, 1999.

Sharma, O. P. "Illustrated Ramayana." In: *Indian and Foreign Review* 17.14 (May 1–14, 1980), 22–23.

Shulman, David. "Divine order and divine evil in the Tamil tale of Rama." In: *Journal of Asian Studies* 38 (1979), 651–69.

Simha, Rajeshwar. "Rāmakathākā vaidika srota." In: *Kalyāṇa* 53.6 (1979), 216–18.

Singh, Atamjit. "Rama kavya tradition in northern India." In: 7.1–2 (Mar.–Sept. 1983), 75–83.

Smith, H. Daniel. *Reading the Ramayana: a bibliographic guide for students and college teachers*. Indian variants on the Rama-theme in English translations. Syracuse, N.Y.: Maxwell School of Citizenship and Public Affairs, Syracuse University, 1983.

—. *The picturebook Ramayana: an illustrated version of Valmiki's story*. Syracuse, N.Y.: Maxwell School of Citizenship and Public Affairs, Syracuse University, 1981.

—. *Valmiki Ramayana in pictures*. Madras: Higginbothams, 1981.

Smith, William L. *Ramayana traditions in eastern India: Assam, Bengal, Orissa*. 2nd ed. New Delhi: Munshiram Manoharlal, 1995.

Sohnen, Renate, ed. 6. 2 vols. 1–2. Reinbek: Inge Wezler, Verlag für orientalistische Fachpublikationen, 1979.

—. "Die Sage des Ramayana: Beobachtungen zur 'Inhaltsangabe' in Buch I, Kap. 1 des Ramayana von Valmiki." In: *Studien zur Indologie und Iranistik* 4 (1978), 54–78.

Stasik, Danuta. *The infinite story: past and present of the Rāmāyaṇas in Hindi*. New Delhi: Manohar Publishers & Distributors, 2009.

Stietencron, Heinrich von, Peter Flamm, John Leonard Brockington, et al. *Epic and Purāṇic bibliography: up to 1985, annotated and with indexes*. Purāṇa research publications, Tübingen 3. Wiesbaden: Otto Harrassowitz, 1992.

Sutton, Nicholas G. "Asoka and Yudhisthira: A historical setting for the ideological tensions of the Mahabharata?" In: *Religion* 27 (Oct. 1997), 333–41.

The Forest Book of the Ramayana of Kampan. Trans. by George L. Hart and Hank Heifetz. Berkeley; London: University of California Press, 1988. [Reprint: 1989.]

Tiwari, Gopinath. "Vedon men Rāmakathā." In: *Avadh University Research Journal* 1.1 (1982), 1–7.

Upadhyay, Ram Bihari. "Rāma kī aitihāsikatā." In: *Avadh University Research Journal* 1.1 (1982), 143–48.

Vijayan, K., ed. *Ramayana in palm leaf pictures: citraramayana*. Trivandrum Sanskrit Series 265. Kariavattom (Trivendrum): Oriental Research Institute & Manuscripts Library, University of Kerala, 1997.

Vyasa, Lallana Prasada, ed. *Ramayana: around the world*. Delhi: B. R. Publishing Corp., 1997.

—. *Ramayana: international perspective*. Delhi: B. R. Publishing Corp., 1998.

—. ed. *The Ramayana: global view*. New Delhi: Har-Anand Publications, 1995.

Wadley, Susan Snow and Priti Ramamurthy, eds. *Spotlight on Ramayana: an enduring tradition*. New York: American Forum for Global Education, 1995.

Whitaker, Jarrod. "Divya astras (divine weapons) and tejas (fiery energy) in the Mahabharata and Ramayana." M.A. diss. University of Canterbury, 1998.

Williams, Joanna Gottfried. *The two-headed deer: illustrations of the Ramayana in Orissa*. California studies in the history of art 34. Berkeley: University of California Press, 1996.

Zieme, Peter. "Ein uigurisches Fragment der Rama Erzahlung." In: *Acta Orientalia Academiae Scientiarum Hungaricae* 32 (1978), 23–32.

6. Other references

Bamber, C. J. *Plants of the Punjab: a descriptive key to the flora of the Punjab, North-west Frontier Province and Kashmir*. Lahore, 1916.

Cowen, D. V. *Flowering trees and shrubs in India*. Bombay: Thacker & Co., 1950.

Dash, Bhagwan. *Materia medica of Ayurveda: based on Madanapāla's Nighaṇṭu*. New Delhi: B. Jain Publishers, 1991.

Mani, Vettam. *Purāṇic encyclopedia*. Delhi: Motilal Banarsidass, 1975.

Mehendale, Madhukar Anant, ed. *Mahābhārata cultural index: being a comprehensive subject-wise index to the cultural information available in the critically constituted text of the Mahābhārata*. 3 vols. Pune: Bhandarkar Oriental Research Institute, 1993–2003.

Printz, Wilhelm. "Bhāṣā-Wörter in Nīlakaṇṭha's Bhāratabhāvadīpa und in anderen Sanskrit-Kommentaren." In: *Zeitschrift für vergleichende Sprachforschung auf dem Gebiete der indogermanischen Sprachen* 44 (1911), 69–109.

Raghavan, V. *Yantras or mechanical contrivances in ancient India*. Indian Institute of Culture, Trans. 10. Bangalore: Indian Institute of Culture, 1952.

Ray, Manmatha Natha. *An index to the proper names occurring in Vālmīki's Rāmāyaṇa*. The Princess of Wales Sarasvati Bhavana Studies (Reprint Series) 5. Varanasi: Sampurnanand Sanskrit Vishvavidyalaya, 1984.

Singh, Thakur Balwant and K. C. Chunekar. *Glossary of vegetable drugs in Bṛhattrayī*. Varanasi: Chowkhamba, 1972.

Sorensen, Soren. *An index to the names in the Mahabharata*. Delhi: Motilal Banarsidass, 1963.

The Mādhavanidāna and its chief commentary: chapters 1–10. Trans. by Gerrit Jan Meulenbeld. Leiden: E. J. Brill, 1974.

www.ingramcontent.com/pod-product-compliance
Lightning Source LLC
Chambersburg PA
CBHW022011160426
43197CB00007B/382
9781943135127